LINUX

COMMAND LINE

*Beginners Guide to Learn Linux
Commands and Shell Scripting*

David A. Williams

TABLE OF CONTENTS

Introduction

I decided to write this book to ease the hurdles that newbie Linux users face. I want you to understand your computer in a better way than you did before. This book contains a complete package for beginners to understand what the Linux operating system is and how it differs from other operating systems. Linux offers you a great learning experience. You can understand the system configuration by skimming a couple of text files that are fully readable. Just remember the individual status of each component and its role when you put together the bigger picture. That's it. Confused. Don't worry. Keep reading until the end of the book and you will understand.

Why should Linux be preferred over other operating systems?

This is what should be answered at the beginning so that you can have the stimulus while you walk through the upcoming chapters of this book. Look, we are not living in the '80s or the '90s. The world has changed so much over the past few years and with it has changed the cyber world. Now all the continents are connected to one another through computer networks. From the oldest to the youngest, all users have access to the Internet. In the nooks and crannies of this cyber world there are humongous data bases that are developed by big businesses. There are billions of web pages that are processing information on a per second basis.

Coupled with these facts are the dangers linked to this ubiquitous connectivity. This is the age when you need a computer on which you have customized applications and complete control. Would you hand over control of your computer system to other companies who keep making a profit by marketing how easy they have made the use of computers? Or would you rather have more freedom and control over your own computer? You deserve freedom to customize control over your computer. You deserve to build your own software for your computer systems. That's why you should prefer Linux over all the other operating systems. With Linux on your computer, you can direct your computer to do as you wish. It will act on your commands.

Command line is the best option

We are trapped in the ease of using computers. We are given attractive graphical user interfaces to deal with which have made us lazy and robbed us of innovation and creativity. This should be done away with. The mouse is not the way to run a computer. It is the keyboard which makes you an expert in using computers. Linux differs from other operating systems in a sense that it offers the Command Line Interface (CLI) instead of the Graphical User Interface. When we talk of the Command Line Interface (CLI), the first thing that comes to the mind of most people is a dark screen. For most people, it is a horrible thought as compared to using a graphical user interface, but this is where your power starts. The CLI allows you greater freedom to talk to your computer and direct it to do certain tasks. You enter commands on the CLI and the computer interprets them and executes them. While the command line interface seems difficult to use - which it no doubt is - it makes difficult tasks easier and faster.

Who should read this book?

You don't have to be a master of programming to read this book. This book is for beginners who are thinking of dipping their toes into

2

the world of Linux. What I expect from you before you go on to the next chapters is a basic understanding of computers. It means that you should be able to tinker with the graphical user interface and finish some key tasks. You should know about booting, startup, log in, files and directories. You should know how to create, save and edit documents and how to browse the web space. But the most important thing of all is your will to learn new things. I'll take you from there.

This book also is for those who are fed up with other operating systems and want to switch to a smarter operating system. I'll tell you about Sylvia, my friend, in the latter chapters, who was forced by her boss to learn Linux for execution of key office tasks. I'll tell the tale of how hard it was for her and how she achieved such a gigantic goal.

If you have just come to know about Linux and want to switch to this unique operating system, this book is definitely for you. Read it, learn the command line and get started.

Before starting the journey, you should bear in mind that there is no shortcut to mastering Linux. Like all great and exciting things, learning Linux takes time. It may turn out to be challenging at times, and may also take great effort on your part. The command line is simple. Also, you can easily remember the commands and the syntax. What makes it tough to master is its broadness. It is so wide to grasp in a short time. But as with all big things, practice makes you perfect. If you keep persevering, you will be able to learn its use and apply it accordingly. The only thing I demand from you as a beginner determination, the ability to tackle failure, and a responsible attitude. A casual approach is not the best way to tackle Linux when you are trying to learn.

What this book has to offer

This book is filled with material that is easy to read and practice, and perfectly suits starters. It is like learning from a tutor. Every step is explained with the help of a command line exercise and a solution for you to understand the process.

- The first section explains what the shell is. You will learn about the different components of the Linux system. In addition, there will be various commands to enter in the shell window for your immediate practice. This section also explains how to navigate the filesystem and different directories in a Linux operating system.

- The second section will take you further into the command line by explaining more about the commands. You will also be able to create your own commands.

- The third section is packed with more details about the Linux environment and system configuration. It will explain how GRUB works on Linux. You will learn about the system startup, the *init* and different runlevels of Linux.

- The fourth section talks about the package management, the repositories and the dependencies. It educates on managing the existing file systems and creating new ones. In addition, it fully explains how you can handle the storage devices using a Linux operating system. You will find an example of editing a partiti0n and altering its type with the help of command line tools.

- The fifth section carries details on the Linux environment variables.

- In the sixth section, you will learn the basics of shell scripting. This is like writing your own software. You will learn about key scripting techniques by which you can control your computer like teaching your computer about decision-making. It is almost akin to artificial intelligence. Your computer will act on its own following a set of instructions. Furthermore, you will learn about some important commands like the case statements, the break statement and the continue statement.

- The final section will take you to the advanced level of shell scripting.

Pre-requisites for reading the book

You will need an operational Linux system on your computer before starting to read this book because it carries practical exercises and their solutions for you.

You can install Linux on your computer. There are a number of distributions, like Fedora, OpenSUSE and Ubuntu. Installing the distribution system is very easy if done in the right way. Of course, there are some specifications that you must have on your computer. For instance, at least 256 MB RAM and around 6GB free space on the hard disk. The higher the specifications of the system the better it is for the operations. It is recommended that you use a personal computer and a landline internet connection. Wireless systems are not suitable for the job.

You can also use the Linux distribution system from a live CD, so there is no need to install it on the system. That's less messy, to say the least. It is easier to do that. On the startup, enter the setup menu and change the boot settings. Switch your boot option to boot from a CD instead of the hard disk. After that insert the CD and you are all ready to use the Linux distribution system. You can run Ubuntu and Fedora from a live CD.

How this book can help you

This book is pretty helpful for those who want to wrap up administrative tasks in a faster way using the Linux environment. You will be able to write your own scripts in order to accomplish specific tasks. After reading this book, you will be able to automate certain administrative tasks with the help of shell scripts. File management, statistical data management and complex arithmetic functions will be a lot easier after you understand some key Linux commands.

CHAPTER 1

Starting with the Linux Shell

Linux is everywhere from our cell phones to computers. Linux got started in the mid '90s. Within a very small window of time, it spread across many industries. Stock markets and super computers also use this operating system. Its popularity is unparalleled. Linux is basically an operating system just like any other, which means it manages the software you install on your system and manages the communication between different pieces of hardware. Seems interesting yet! Let's roll on.

What is Linux?

Before moving on to the complex parts, it is better that you sail through the basic world of Linux first. For beginners, understanding Linux can be perplexing if they don't know what Linux actually is and what it offers.

Though it may appear complex and undoable thing at the start, in reality, it is easier to learn than you may think. The Linux operating system consists of the following parts.

Bootloader: This manages the boot process of a computer. You might have seen a splash screen coming and going in the blink of an eye before you boot into the operating system.

The Kernel: This is also dubbed as the core of the system. It manages the entire system by deploying software and hardware when they are needed. In addition, the kernel manages system memory, as well as the file system.

The Shell: You can give directions to your computer by typing commands in the form of texts. This command line is dubbed as the shell which is the daunting part of Linux. People just don't want to venture into it. My friend Sylvia never liked Linux until her boss pushed her into this uncanny tech world. Once she got into it, she loved it more than Windows and Mac. The control the command line gave her made her quite comfortable with it at her office. The shell allowed her to copy, move and rename files with the help of the command prompt. All the struggle she had to go through was memorizing the text commands and the rest of it was the easy part. The command prompt does everything. You can type in a program name to start it. The shell sends the relevant info to the kernel, and it does the rest of the execution.

Getting Started

After you have installed Linux, create a regular user to run as your personal account. Log in to the account.

The Shell Window

The shell is an integral part of the command line. The command line, in reality, is the shell itself. In simple words it takes keyboard commands as input and then processes them toward the operating system for execution. Different Graphical User Interfaces (GUIs) use different terminal emulators which allow you to put in text commands through the shell. Some newbies get confused by the large number of emulators available online. To clear your mind, just remember that the basic job of all terminal emulators is to give you a gateway to the shell. One more thing: a terminal emulator is also known as the shell window.

Unix also uses a shell system, but Linux has the same system, but it's better. This enhanced version of the shell is dubbed as "bash" which comes as a default shell on most of the Linux distributions.

After you have launched the emulator, the screen will show you something like the following:

For Ubuntu users it will look like: aka@localhost ~$

```
For Fedora users it appears like: [aka@localhost ~]$
```

This text is known as the shell prompt in which aka is the username while 'localhost' denotes the machine name. Their values may differ. Usually, the $ sign accompanies you all the time you are in the shell window. If you see the sign of #, it means you are logged in as a root user or the emulator you are using offers super user privileges. If this is your first time with Linux, just open the DOS command prompt on the windows. You will have the same experience while using the shell window. There is not much difference except for the commands. The environment is more or less alike.

Do you want to type something on your screen? Let's do that.

```
[aka@localhost ~]$ tera
```

Did you write your name? Write it down. The shell will analyze the command and respond with the following:

```
bash: tera : command not found
[aka@localhost ~]$
```

You cannot use a mouse on the emulator. Instead, the keyboard arrows will help you do some magic. Strike the upper arrow key to scroll through the history of your commands. The downward arrow will bring you to the latest command. Also, the previous command disappears while you get down to the new one. Isn't it like the DOS

Command prompt? The right and left arrows will help you to position the cursor in order to edit the command if need be.

Just stay right there and try some simple commands.

```
[aka@localhost ~]$ date

Thus Aug 15 12:18:01 UTC 2019

[aka@localhost ~]$
```

If you type down 'cal' in place of 'date,' a full month's calendar will be displayed on the screen.

Basic Commands

If you are looking forward to operating Linux just like Windows, you are wrong. Linux is smarter. You get to work with a command set. It is just like coding. Enter the command to get the job done, and that's it. Let's see which of these you can operate. The fun is going to start from here. Get ready!

The marvel of the echo command is as under.

```
[root@localhost ~]# echo My love
My love
```

The # sign indicates that I am logged in as a *root* user. I think we are done with that. Now enter the following:

Let's try the cat comman-d and see what it can do.

```
[aka@localhost ~]$ cat/etc/passwd
```

A huge number of rows and columns will appear below the command. This command is meant to display the contents of the above file.

Do you want to move files from one place to another? Check out the *mv* command.

10

```
[aka@localhost ~]$ mv downloads documents
```

```
[aka@localhost ~]$ mv documents downloads programs lib
```

With the help of the second command, you can move multiple files at the same time into a particular directory. In the above command, *lib* denotes the name of the directory.

The cp command is used to copy files in Linux from one place to another like from downloads to documents.

```
[aka@localhost ~]$ cp downloads documents
```

```
[aka@localhost ~]$ cp file1 file2 file3 file4 fileN dir
```

The second command is to copy content from multiple files into a single directory.

With the help of the *touch* command, you can create a file. If the file already exists on your computer, its time stamp will be modified.

```
[aka@localhost ~]$ touch video
[aka@localhost ~]$ ls -1 video
```

As you enter the second command, it will show the modified time of the respective file.

In the end, *rm* command is used to delete files from the system. Is the recycle bin going through your mind? Forget it. You don't have to search the file manually to dispatch it to the recycle bin. Just type *rm* and the file name. It will be removed.

```
[aka@localhost ~]$ rm downloads
```

The text 'downloads' is the name of the file.

Just like the *touch* command, you can also create a new directory by typing *mkdir* and the new directory's name.

```
[aka@localhost ~]$ mkdir lib
[aka@localhost ~]$ cd /lib
[aka@localhost lib]$
```

Congratulations! You have succeeded in creating a new file. Here *mk* denotes make.

rmdir command allows you to remove a directory. Here *rm* denotes remove.

```
[aka@localhost ~]$ rmdir lib
```

The file will be removed from the system right away. You must keep in mind that the *lib* directory should not be empty at the time of removal, otherwise, the command will fail. This is perfect for you if you are one of those people who are sick of deleting individual files after searching out hundreds of folders and files. It will delete entire directories.

'What if I want to delete the sub directories that exist in the main directory?' asked Sylvia, who had by now learned enough to be able to craft a question after hours of brainstorming. For that purpose, you can add -rf to the command was my reply.

```
[aka@localhost ~]$ rm -rf lib
```

Although this command is a really helpful one for your businesses or personal work, this can also be a very lethal one. It can delete humongous amounts of data in the blink of an eye. Make sure you are deleting the right directory before executing the command. Once you enter it, it is all gone.

Let's take a look the options we have with the *rm* command.

rm documents : it helps you delete a particular file named 'documents.'

Rm -i documents   : type this in the window and you will be asked for confirmation before deleting the file

Rm -r documents lib : it will delete the *documents* file and *lib* directory along with the contents.

rm -rf documents lib : this also deletes the *documents* file and *lib* directory even if one of them doesn't exist. The point is that it doesn't fail considering the fact that what you wrote as a file name didn't exist in the system.

The *In* command

This command creates new links. You can use it in the following forms:

```
[aka@localhost ~]$ In file link
[aka@localhost ~]$ ls -s item link (for hard link)
```

Managing the System's Memory

Memory in Linux is divided into blocks, technically known as pages. When you enter a command to locate a particular page or general information on the memory of the system, the kernel starts working to gather the blocks into columns with each section designation a particular kind of memory like total memory, used memory and free memory. There is a process dubbed as swapping out, executed by the kernel in which it accesses the memory pages that remain out of access and brings them down to the swap space. Now the question on your mind may be whether the kernel does that when you are out of memory. Well, no, it doesn't. It does that randomly. So, the swap space remains filled all the time. If you run a program that needs a block which the kernel has swapped out, it starts creating space for it. Yes, you understood this. The kernel swaps out some other page to bring in the required page.

If you want to check the memory on your Linux system, there are specific commands to do that. Some of them are as shown below, both for checking the swap as well as the RAM memory:

The free command: Let's start right away. You will see the following table:

```
[aka@localhost ~]$ free

          total              used   free   buffers     cached
Mem:   7976               5000   2976   749         1918

-/+ buffers/cache:        xxx    yyy
Swap            xxx       yyy    zzz
```

The table is self-explanatory. Everything is explained with the help of columns. You get to know about the total, used and free memory. It also shows memory consumption by buffers and cache, and also the status of the swap memory.

The df command: You can easily see the free space on your hard drive by the following simple command.

```
[root@localhost ~]# df

Filesystem    1k-blocks    used      Available    Use%
Mounted on
/dev/root     1048576      207640    840936 20%/
devtmpfs      125948       0         125948       0% /dev
tmpfs         125988       8         125980       0% /run

[root@localhost ~]#
```

The proc/ meminfo file: Another popular method to check the memory status is reading the proc/meminfo file.

Type in the command: '$ cat/proc/meminfo' and you will see a long list of options along with details of the memory consumed by each of them. Let's see. The following columns will pop up on your screens when you put in the commands.

```
[root@localhost ~]# $ cat/proc/meminfo

MemTotal:                        xxx                    kb
MemFree:                xxx                              kb
Buffers:                xxx                              kb
Cached:                 xxx                              kb
SwapCached:                      xxx                    kb
Active:                          xxx                    kb
Inactive:               xxx                              kb
Active(anon):                    xxx                    kb
Inactive (anon):                 xxx                    kb
Active(file):                    xxx                    kb
Inactive(file):                          xxx            kb
Unevictable:                     xxx                    kb
Mlocked:                xxx                              kb
SwapTotal:                       xxx                    kb
SwapFree:               xxx                              kb
Dirty:                           xxx                    kb
Writeback:                       xxx                    kb
AnonPages:                       xxx                    kb
Mapped:                 xxx                              kb
Shmem:          xxx                                      kb
Slab:                   xxx                              kb
SReclaimable:           xxx                              kb
SUnrelcaim:             xxx                              kb
PageTables:             xxx                              kb
NFS_Unstable:   xxx                                      kb
Bounce:         xxx                                      kb
Commitlimit:            xxx                              kb
Committed_AS:   xxx                                      kb
VmallocTotal:           xxx                              kb
VmallocUsed:            xxx                              kb
VmallocChunk:   xxx                                      kb
HubPages_Total:         xxx                              kb
HubPages_Free:  xxx                                      kb
HubPages_Rsvd:  xxx                                      kb
HubPages_Surp:  xxx                                      kb
Hubpagesize:            xxx                              kb


#
```

This memory detail shows the total memory line of physical memory that the Linux server has. How much is used and where it is used will be shown. You can see all the memory pages which can differ from system to system. Your Linux system might not have created some of the above-mentioned pages.

An Overview of Navigation in the Shell

You will easily get bored with Linux if you get stuck in a single spot. You must be able to navigate through different files and directories to enjoy your experience with this one of a kind operating system. You need to get an idea of where you are and what things you have access to and with which command you can access them. First of all, you should know where your feet are. To learn this, use the following command.

```
[aka@localhost ~]$ pwd
```

In most cases, people land in the home directory of their accounts. Now, what is the home directory? Let me explain it all. A home directory is a place where you can store your files in addition to building up directories. You are the boss here. It is like a real home for you. Feel free to store your data here and also create multiple directories. In the command 'pwd' p means print, w means working, and d is for directory.

Is it a tree?

It doesn't look like one, but it is one, for sure. As in the Windows operating system Linux arranges all its files and folders into a hierarchical structure. Yes, it looks like a tree if you could somehow materialize it into something concrete. Hence the need for the word 'tree.' You may be fascinated to know that things are mostly the same among different operating systems such as Windows and Linux. The creators changed some names to differentiate these systems for the ease of users. For example, what is called a directory in Linux, is commonly known as a folder in Windows.

Let me take you further into the world of Linux directories. First of all, these directories become a bit different from Windows' folders in a way that they can carry a large number of files as well as subdirectories. The very first directory you are confronted with is the 'root' directory.

Where Linux doesn't agree with Windows

Well, disagreements happen in the world. If you are a Windows user, you are most used to an individual filing system for the hard drive, USB storage device and DVD drives. But Linux has defied this system. It offers a single treelike filing system for all the external and internal storage devices.

Windows made things easier for an average user that detached us from the relish of complex technical commands. Look, Windows presents the filing system, of course, in the form of a tree, in a graphical fashion. There are many plus signs and negative signs. With the pluses, you can further explore the branches of the tree while the minuses help you close up those branches and simplify the view. The root always remains at the top.

If you are thinking about something as cool as a graphical outlook, stop thinking right now. Linux makes it fun by offering you the potential to navigate through different files and folders with the help of putting in text commands. In the Linux terminal or shell window, you are always in one or another directory that is called the current directory. To know your exact position 'pwd' command helps you as I have explained earlier.

Do you want to know about the contents of the directory? Everybody does. I believe that you have already learned, as well as practiced knowing the directory you are currently in. Time to delve deeper into the system. You should know how to explore the contents of the directory with a single command. Either you can stay in the home directory and explore it, or you can move to your favorite one. To explore the directory you are currently working in, try the following command.

```
[aka@localhost ~]$ ls
Pictures Videos Games Documents
```

My friend Sylvia loves to jump from one folder to another at the speed of light. While it is fun to do this in Windows, it is faster and easier to do in Linux. Just remember the 'cd' factor. Sylvia learned it, though the hard way, by jotting it down in her notebook and memorizing the entire text. Now she just types 'cd' and the pathname of the directory she wants to jump into.

Let me confess it is not as simple as it looks. The pathname is like a magic circle in which we jump to reach the directory we want to be in. Pathnames fall into two categories: relative and absolute. Shall we deal with the 'absolute' first?

Absolute pathnames: Also known as absolute path or a full path. A pathname is usually made up with the sequence of characters, containing the name of the object. The name of the directory in which it rests is also part of the name. There can be a directory that contains software and programs. In this directory, there are other directories to which you need access. Your path will be like the following.

```
[aka@localhost ~]$ cd/ usr/lib
[aka@localhost lib]$
```

You can at any time confirm if you have actually moved to the desired directory by applying the 'pwd' command.

Relative Pathnames: You can start from the current directory and move to the parent directory with a simple command. Do you love to

18

put in dots like (....). A single dot refers to the current working directory whole the double (..) leads you to the parent directory.

```
[aka@localhost ~]$ cd/ usr/lib
[aka@localhost lib]$
```

I want to go to the /usr. You can do that either the long way or the shorter way. Let's do this first the longer but safer way.

```
[aka@localhost lib]$ cd/ usr
[aka@localhost usr]$ pwd
/usr
```

Now do this the shorter and the faster way.

```
[aka@localhost lib]$ cd..
[aka@localhost usr]$ pwd
/usr
```

Done. You have switched it to the parent directory. Wait. We are not all done on this. Let's get back to the working directory once again by two methods. We are currently in the parent directory. Remember that. Your screen is currently showing the following.

```
[aka@localhost usr]$
```

Type the following.

```
[aka@localhost usr]$ cd/ usr/lib
[aka@localhost lib]$
```

Let's do this in a shorter and faster way. Do you remember what single dot was supposed to do?

```
[aka@localhost usr]$ cd./bin
[aka@localhost lib]$
```

Sylvia just hated the dots. She always put doubles where she had to insert the single and single where a double was needed. One day, when I was taking a quick walk by her office, I dropped in and found her messed up with these simple commands. A friend in need is a friend indeed. I told her a magic formula for switching from parent directory to the working directory. Let's try that.

```
[aka@localhost usr]$ cd bin
[aka@localhost bin]$
```

Not only are the dots omitted but also the slashes.

A trick of the trade: cd is an abbreviation of current and directory. If you try out just the cd command, it will bounce you back to the directory in which you first started after you logged in.

```
[aka@localhost lib]$ cd
[aka@localhost ~]$
```

More on the 'cd' command: Let's try out the (-). It is supposed to change the working directory to the one you left behind. Suppose you are currently in lib after switching from the 'usr'.

```
[aka@localhost lib]$ cd -
/usr
[aka@localhost usr]$
```

Another important command to know is cd ~ username. If you have another user name like john, you can put in the name in the place of username to switch to that account's directory.

Food for thought: It is important to keep in mind that in Linux you need to take care that you are using the right case when you are entering a file name in the shell window. In this operating system downloads and Downloads are two different things.

If at any time you want to go back up where you started, just type *cd* and press enter. Then enter *pwd* to know where you are at the moment.

What you can already do with the ls Command

It is now time to learn more commands as you already know the basics. You now know that ls is used to list directories. Also, you can view the content of the directories.

```
[aka@localhost ~]$ ls
bin  games  include  lib  lib64  libexec  local  sbin
share  src  tmp
```

In the above command, you can see four different directories. Now I want you to take a dive into your brain and bring out a specific directory name you want to list. Let me dive in first using mine. I'll use # for this command - that is the face of the super user.

```
[aka@localhost ~]$ ls /usr
```

Let us take a look at some more options for the ls command.

There is an option (- a) which can be extended to --all. It will list all files including the ones starting from a period that usually remain hidden from other commands.

```
[aka@localhost ~]$ ls -a
. ..  bin  games  include  lib  lib64  libexec  local
sbin  share  src  tmp
```

The second option is -d that can be extended to --directory. If used alone, this command will show you a list of your directory's contents. You can pair it up with the -1 in order to view the content details.

The third option to consider is the -1 command. You can see the outcomes in the long form.

```
[aka@localhost ~]$ ls -1
bin
games
include
```

21

```
lib
lib64
libexec
local
sbin
share
src
tmp
```

The fourth option is the -S. It sorts out the results with respect to the size of the file. Here S denotes the word size. If you remember the signs by assigning them a full, relevant and familiar word, it will help you memorize the commands faster than normal.

The fifth option is -h with the long form --human-readable. This helps you to get a full-size display of directories and files that is human-readable instead of just showing bytes.

The sixth option is -r with the long form --reverse. It displays your results in a reverse angle that means in the descending alphabetical order.

```
[aka@localhost ~]$ ls -r

tmp   src   share   sbin   local   libexec   lib64   lib   incl
ude   games   bin
```

The seventh option is -t. As apparent from the use of the letter 't' this option offers to view the results with respect to modification of time.

```
[aka@localhost ~]$ ls -t
sbin   lib   lib64   libexec   share   include   src   local
games   tmp   bin
```

You can see that the position of the files has been changed with respect to the modification of time.

How to make out a File's Type

Now that we are going deeper into the system, it is time to know how to determine the type of a particular file. Actually, Linux does not make it that much easy for the users as Windows does. There are not familiar and most likely type file names that you could easily guess. It makes it rough and tough. To determine a file type, you should type in the following command.

```
[aka@localhost ~]$ file downloads
```

This is known as the file command. When you execute it, it is likely to print the following information.

```
[aka@localhost ~]$ file downloads
images.jpg: JFIF standard 1.01
```

In Linux there are lots of files. As you explore the system, you get to know more and more types of the files. So, stay tuned! Keep reading.

The *Less* Command

There is another important command in the arsenal of Linux that is the *less* command. It is a full program for those who are interested in viewing text files. This command helps you view the human-readable files in your system. It tracks them out in no time and allows you to view them.

Wait! As I write, Sylvia knocks the door and jumps in the lounge where I was working on my laptop. She is always curious about learning the Linux command line since the day her boss made it mandatory for her to do that. I must admit that what was earlier on a big burden on her nerves and shoulders had now turned into a passion. She loves the way Linux made it easier to wrap up office work in lesser time. The time she saves at the office allows her to drop in at her friends' homes. I hope you have stopped thinking about why she is here in my home. Let's welcome her.

Sylvia, when learning the *less* command, was always curious why do we need this command in the first place? In fact, why do we need to see the text files? Its answer is that many files are not just ordinary files. They are system files that contain *configuration files*. They are stored in your system in this special format.

If you are thinking like Sylvia, you might say that's not a big deal. Why do I have to view the configuration files in the first place? There is an answer to that as well. This command not only shows the system file but also lots of real programs that your system is using. These programs are technically called *scripts*. They are always stored in the system in this specific format.

I am using the word *text* for quite some time. Information can be displayed on a computer in a variety of forms. It is represented in the form of pictures, videos, numbers and alphabets in Windows operating system. Normally the language that the computer understands is in numerical form like the binary digits.

If we look at text as the representation system, it feels simpler and easier than all the other methods. The human brain processes the information faster than in this form. Numbers are converted into text one-by-one. This system is very compact. This text is different from that of the one in word processors. I am telling you about this because in Linux a number of files are stored in the system in the form of text files. Let's see how can we use the *less* command.

[aka@localhost ~]$ less downloads

This program helps users to navigate through a specific file. Some files are longer and some are shorter. For longer files, such as the one containing system information, it can be scrolled up and down.

If you want to exit the less command just strike the Q key. Some files can be really longer like the following one.

```
[aka@localhost ~]$ less /etc/passwd
```

Things to Remember

You can use the `PageUP` key to scroll back a page. Use 'b' instead if you don't like to use `PageUP`.

Use the `PageDn` key to scroll on to the next page. For the same purpose, you can also use spacebar.

The up arrow and down arrow keys are used for moving to one line above and below respectively.

If you are in the middle of the text and want to jump to the end of the text file, press G. To reach the start of the text file, press 1G or g.

'h' can be used to get the help screen displayed.

'q' is always there to quit the *less* command.

Common Directory Names in Linux

'/' denotes the root. There are usually no files in this directory.

'/lib/' denotes the library directory to store library files.

/root takes you to the home directory. A root user is also called the super user.

/etc contains configuration files

/bin stores GNU user-level utilities. Also known as the binary directory.

/opt is executed to store optional software.

/dev is known as the device directory.

/usr is the user installed software directory

/var is the variable directory. It changes frequently.

CHAPTER 2

◆·+·◆·+·◆·+·◆·+·◆————————◆·+·◆

Exploring the Realm of Commands

I hope that by now, you have gained sufficient knowledge about how you can navigate through the shell window using simple commands. That's easy, you see. A little bit of extra consideration will help you get through most of the work in no time which in the Windows operating system might have taken hours of exhaustive work. One more interesting thing is that the commands are easy to memorize. You can also create your own commands and that's what we will learn in this chapter. Also, by getting acquainted with more commands, you will feel more comfortable in using them in the real shell window.

There are different types of commands:

It can be a shell function, a kind of shell scripts that are incorporated in the environment. Commands constitute executable programs just like software engineers do while working on C language or Python and Ruby. Or a command can be an alias which is your self-made command.

Do you know how to know a command's type? Let' see how it is done.

```
[aka@localhost ~]$ type cd
cd is a shell buildin
```

```
[aka@localhost ~]$ type cp
cp is /bin/cp
[aka@localhost ~]$ type rm
rm is /bin/rm
[aka@localhost ~]$ type mkdir
mkdir is /bin/mkdir
```

Now we know the type of each of our commands.

The *Which* Command

You can use this command to track the executable file. On Linux systems, unlike the Windows operating system, more than one version of programs are installed. This command tells us where to find the program.

Let's look at the syntax:

```
-/bin/cd
[aka@localhost ~]$ which rm
/bin/rm
```

It doesn't work on built in programs. See the following syntax.

```
[aka@localhost ~]$ which ls

/usr/bin/which: no ls in
(/usr/local/sbin:/bin:/sbin:/usr/bin:/usr/sbin:/usr/loc
al/bin)
```

The info which command: this command displays the help information.

```
[aka@localhost ~]$ info which

Next: Which Program, Prev (dir),     Up: (dir)

'which': Show the full path of commands

******************************************
```

The 'which' program shows the full path of (shell) commands.

This file documents 'which' version 2.21, updated 20 March 2015.

*Menu:

*Which Program::	The 'which' Program
*Invoking Which::	How to invoke 'which'
*Option Summary::	Overview of commandline options
*Return Value::	The return value of 'which'
*Example::	Examples of invocation
*Bugs::	Known bugs
*See Also::	Related UNIX commands
*Index::	Index

----Info: (which)Top, 20 lines --All------------------

Welcome to Infor version 6.5. Type H for help, h for tutorial.

If you type H, the following details show up on your screen.

```
Basic Info command keys


H      Close this help window

q      Quit Info altogether

h      Invoke the Info tutorial


Up     Move up the Info tutorial

Down   Move down one line

PgUp   Scroll backward one screenful.

PgDn   Scroll forward one screenful.

Home   Go to the beginning of this node.

End    Go to the end of this node.


-----Info: *Info Help*, 302 lines --Top----------------
```

Now type *h* and the following details will appear on your screens.

```
Next: Help-P,   Prev: Help-Small-Screen,   Up: Getting Started
```

The *Help* Command

You have learned lots of commands and their solutions. It is time to know the command that can get you out of the mess if you are stuck in the middle of the course and don't know what to do. Sylvia loved this feature while she was in the learning phase. One day I was planning to celebrate my daughter's birthday at a beach-side resort, Sylvia phoned me. She was panicked as she had messed up some command at her office computer. She tried the *help* command but to no avail. When the *help* command failed to do its job, she panicked. Actually, the *help* command is only created for the shell built-ins.

```
[aka@localhost ~]$ help cd

cd: cd [-L|[-P [-e]] [-@]] [dir]

    Change the shell working directory.
```

An interesting thing about the *help* command is to get to know what the command has to offer inside the shell window. Let's see the syntax.

```
[aka@localhost ~]$ help help

help: help [-dms] [pattern ...]

    Display information about builtin commands.
```

The --*help* Option

This command will help you explore more information about executable programs. This one is really amazing because it shows different options pertaining to the program and also the supported syntax. It becomes easier to learn and exercise more commands on the go. You don't need to consult a book for small hurdles.

```
[aka@localhost ~]$ cp --help
```

The help feature can also be used along with different options to get more information along the way.

Using it with –*d*:

```
[aka@localhost ~]$ help -d help
help - Displays information about built in commands
```

Using it with *–s*:

```
[aka@localhost ~]$ help -s help
help: help [-dms] [pattern ...]
```

The *man* command: In most cases, an executable program offers a formal piece of documentation that is dubbed as a *man page*. You can view the document with the help of the following command.

```
[aka@localhost ~]$ man program
```

Here program refers to the command that you want to view. The pages of *man* are displayed as such that there is a title. There also is a description that explains why should you use a particular command? Beside that there will be lists along with the description of the command's options. Let's dissect a *man printf* command.

```
[aka@localhost ~]$ man printf
```

There will be a name of the document. Below which there will be the heading of SYNOPSIS. Then comes the description. This section carries in-depth details about the options available for the particular program. For the *printf*, *--help* and *–version* are available.

That was about the full page of the manual. It takes a lot of time to skim through the entire pages to locate a particular piece of information. Don't worry. You can type a targeted command to read a particular section of the manual. The *man* command offers you to specify the section number. Let's see how to do it.

```
[aka@localhost ~]$ man section search_term
[aka@localhost ~]$ man 9 passwd
```

When you execute the command, you will reach the specific section of the man page.

The *whatis* Command

If you don't know what a specific command has to offer, you can run the *whatis* command to have a brief detail about it. In most cases, the detail consists of a one liner but self-explanatory so that you learn about the function of the command faster.

```
[aka@localhost ~]$ whatis Is
Is                  (1)    - list directory contents
```

The *info* Command

For the users of GNU Project, there is an alternative to man dubbed as the *info pages*. These pages come with a reader program named as *info*. The syntax runs as follows:

```
[aka@localhost ~]$ info option menu-item
```

An example: the syntax is as under.

```
[aka@localhost ~]$ info -d cvs
```

As I have already told you that Linux stores files in a tree like hierarchical structure. The *info files* in a Linux also are in the form of a tree. They are built into individual nodes. Each one of them contains a single topic. There also are hyperlinks for easy navigation to another node. Well, they are not dyed in blue, just as in Windows. They can be identified by their leading asterisk. Move over the cursor and strike the Enter key to open it.

The *info* command is very interesting to use. You can use it from multiple angles. If you want information on the physical location of the file, the syntax is given as under:

```
[aka@localhost ~]$ info -w cvs
/usr/share/info/cvs/info.gz
```

In case you need information on the options pertaining to a particular command, you can do this by making a simple change in the syntax.

```
[aka@localhost ~]$ info -O mv

Next: rm invocation,  Prev: install invocation,  Up: Ba
sic operations
```

It displays the options node for the *mv* command. You can learn a lot with the help of *info* command. When Sylvia was learning Linux command line, she used to keep a notebook with her to jot down important things they came across while running the shell window. This helped her a lot. She picked up important pieces of information she knew.

Let's look at the options the *info* command has to offer.

- -O takes us to the options available for a particular command line.

- -d, d for directory, helps us add directory to the INFOPATH

- -k finds out STRING in all the indices available in all the manuals.

- -o is about offering selected nodes to the file.

- -version offers users information about the version.

The *apropos* Command

For a normal human being, using Linux is not a child's play. It is not that it is something ethereal which the earthmen don't understand, but it is its commands that make it nothing less than a horrible thought. It is almost a nightmare for me to even think that I had to memorize each command to be a Linux pro. If you are just like me and cannot remember a ton of commands that Linux has to offer, perhaps you need a comprehensive lecture on this very command. It just saves me from lots of hassle of remembering so many commands.

The skilled hands behind the development of Linux also understand this. That's why they have created the *apropos* command. Just a keyword of a command is enough for *apropos* to transport it in front of your eyes. This command helps users to be more efficient and effective when they are at the shell window. Shall we see the syntax now?

```
[aka@localhost ~]$ apropos keyword
[aka@localhost ~]$ apropos option keyword
```

You can use one keyword at a time.

```
[aka@localhost ~]$ apropos email
```

It will display all the necessary information about the email. To add more spice, you can use the option -d which will trigger the terminal to return path& man directories etc. pertaining to the keyword you enter.

```
[aka@localhost ~]$ apropos -d email
```

The list goes on. I have just written a little less than half of the details that the window returned in response to the apropos command.

Are you a Google user? If you are, you might know that google cannot see you in pain of thinking the exact keywords that you need to search. You enter a word and a list drops down containing most relevant search phrases. Most often, I go with one of the phrases from the list. Just imagine if you could avail yourself of a similar facility in Linux. Thankfully, you can. Use the -e option. Let's jump to the syntax right away.

```
[aka@localhost ~]$ apropos -e compress
```

You will have a list of commands starting from the word 'compress.'

A Trick of the Trade

Is it possible to combine different commands and get results? Absolutely, yes. You can do that. I'll write down the syntax.

```
[aka@localhost ~]$ cd /usr; ls; cd -
bin   games   include   lib   lib64   libexec   local   sbin
share   src   tmp
/usr
```

We have successfully executed three consecutive commands in a go; changing the directory to /usr, listing the directory, and then returning to the directory in which we were in before the execution of the command. All three in a command.

Shall we try creating our own commands?

We can do that with the help of the command we have just tried and tested. Think about a possible name and confirm if it has not been taken.

```
[aka@localhost ~]$ type xin
Sh: type; xin; not found
```

So, xin is not there. Here is the syntax to create the alias.

```
[aka@localhost ~]$ alias xin='cd/usr; ls; cd -`
```

Just remember the string and finding out a name that has not already been taken. Execute the command. Great! It seems you have already created your own command.

Let's try the new command.

```
[aka@localhost ~]$ xin
bin   games   include   lib   lib64   libexec   local   sbin
share   src   tmp
/usr
```

Congratulations! To confirm run the *type* command to see to which your command *xin* has been aliased to.

```
[aka@localhost ~]$ type xin
xin is aliased to `cd/usr; ls; cd -'
```

If you desire to take a look at all the aliases in the environment, follow the syntax as under.

```
[aka@localhost ~]$ alias
egrep='egrep --color=auto'
fgrep='fgrep --color=auto'
grep='grep --color=auto'
l.='ls -d .* --color=auto'
ll='ls -l --color=auto'
ls='ls --color=auto'
mc='. /usr/libexec/mc/mc-wrapper.sh'
which='(alias; declare -f) | /usr/bin/which --tty-
only --read-alias --read-funct
ions --show-tilde --show-dot'
xin='cd/usr; ls; cd -'
xzegrep='xzegrep --color=auto'
xzfgrep='xzfgrep --color=auto'
xzgrep='xzgrep --color=auto'
zegrep='zegrep --color=auto'
zfgrep='zfgrep --color=auto'
zgrep='zgrep --color=auto'
```

Your screen can show a slightly different result as per the environment you are using. Just be sure you have the information about aliases that are present in your system.

The I/O Saga

We are going to learn about the input and output in the shell window. You will be using meta characters. Basically, this is responsible for rerouting the I/O between the files. In addition, it is used to create command pipelines.

Getting acquainted with the Standard Stream: Almost all computer-based programs deliver output in reaction to the input you place. For example, if you are browsing through a website and you enter the back button, a window pops up forbidding you from getting back, or you will lose your data. The same kind of window pops up when you try to close a word file that you have not yet saved. You enter keys on the keyboard just like you are going to do right now; its results show on the desktop in a word file or in the Google search bar or in the terminal emulator of Linux. That's how the I/O system runs in general. You do have some error messages placing themselves like a frowning genie at the door of a cave.

Dissecting the I/O System

Standard input: It is given the '0' number. Your keyboard is used for the input. In short form, it will look like this (stdin).

Standard output: It has the (1) number. Your guess is right. Of course, the output is displayed on the screen before your eyes. No doubt about that, you see. In short, it is displayed as (stdout.)

Standard error: Give it the number (2). If you miss something in the input or don't exactly know the command, the bash shell will throw off an error box. It is displayed as (stderr) in short form.

There is nothing complex about the redirection process regarding the relationship between a keyboard and the Windows operating system. You will understand what it is all about.

I want to Redirect toward a File

Redirection is a little bit technical than the other commands, and also a bit different. You will be using > and < brackets. Sometimes you will have to use >> or << brackets for the desired output. But don't worry, we will learn to use this.

Let's roll on. You will have to use the > symbol along with the desired filename. You can dispatch the output of the command to the file you want. Let's learn it in a simple way. You are working in the Microsoft Word. You type in your name but don't want it to be displayed on the screen and instead desire it to be moved to a particular file.

```
[aka@localhost ~]$ echo Hi there. > test.txt
[aka@localhost ~]$ cat test.txt
Hi everyone.
[aka@localhost ~]$
```

The file returns back to you only when you demand.

I want to Erase the Output

Yes, you can. Commands in Linux definitely are like magic wands. With a single and simple command, you can do overwrite the command. Let's do that.

```
[aka@localhost ~]$ cat test.txt
Hi everyone.
[aka@localhost ~]$ leo > test.txt
Sh: leo: command not found
[aka@localhost ~]$ cat test.txt
[aka@localhost ~]$
```

You can see that the file is not found still it was overwritten and erased. When I run the cat command after that, there was no return.

I don't want the file to be erased like that: Do you mean it? Of course, you mean it. There is a way to do that. We have the noclobber option to save deletion due to overwriting of files. Let's learn the syntax .

```
[aka@localhost ~]$ echo I love blue sky. >
mydocuments.txt

[aka@localhost ~]$ cat mydocuments.txt
I love blue sky.
[aka@localhost ~]$ set -o noclobber
[aka@localhost ~]$ echo the sky is azure. >
mydocuments.txt
sh: mydocuments.txt: cannot overwrite existing file
[aka@localhost ~]$ set +o noclobber
[aka@localhost ~]$ echo the sky is azure. >
mydocuments.txt
[aka@localhost ~]$ cat mydocuments.txt
the sky is azure.
```

The first command kept the output from getting overwritten, but the second one reverted it back to the prior position.

The noclobber can be overruled:

Suppose we have the noclobber in place that is preventing the overwriting process. Try this one out.

```
[aka@localhost ~]$ echo the sky is azure. >
mydocuments.txt
sh: mydocuments.txt: cannot overwrite existing file
[aka@localhost ~]$ echo the sky is azure. >|
mydocuments.txt
[aka@localhost ~]$ cat mydocuments.txt
the sky is azure.
```

The sign >| does the magic. Clearly, the noclobber has been overruled.

If you want to redirect two file content without overwriting the first, there is a command for this. As I said, we have magic signs for the purpose. So, let's do that.

```
[aka@localhost ~]$ cat mydocuments.txt
I love blue sky.
[aka@localhost ~]$ echo the sky is azure. >>
```

```
mydocuments.txt
[aka@localhost ~]$ cat mydocuments.txt
I love blue sky
the sky is azure
[aka@localhost ~]$
```

This process is known as *appending*. It makes sense as two file contents are combined in the process.

Redirecting the Error Message

Let's practice this first in the terminal emulator.

```
[aka@localhost ~]$ echo hi everyone
hi everyone
[aka@localhost ~]$ echo hi everyone 2> /dev/null
hi everyone
[aka@localhost ~]$ zcho hi everyone 2> /dev/null
[aka@localhost ~]$
[aka@localhost ~]$ zcho hi everyone
sh: zcho: command not found
[aka@localhost ~]$
```

So, you can see how this command can make our display less messy. There won't be lengthy explanations if you type it wrong. Make sure to keep your display clean in the future.

Moving on to the Pipelines

Your commands are redirected through a network of pipelines. The standard inputs and outputs are received and displayed, respectively, with the help of the pipelines.

| is the operator. It is like a wall that helps pass one output to some other virtual place. It is just like you are transferring some physical commodity. Executing the pipeline command will help you push one output to another command. No activity on the display screen is required neither is required the dull exchange through temp files. A pipe does all the process in the background in complete silence. One

important thing to remember is that you can only send the data. You cannot receive it from the same pipe. The information flows in just one direction. I am using the less command because it displays the standard output of almost all commands. Test it and see the results. The results may differ from user to user.

```
[aka@localhost ~]$ ls -1 /usr/bin | less
[
ack
addr2line
ag
alias
animalsay
animate
annocheck
appliance-creator
applydeltarpm
appstreamcli
apropos
ar
arch
aria2c
arpaname
as
aserver
aulast
aulastlog
ausyscall
authvar
auvirt
awesome
awesome-client
awk
axel
b2sum
```

Redirecting Standard Input

The cat command—Concatenate files

This command is special in that it tends to read one and more than one files. It also moves files and copies them to standard output. Let's see how it runs.

```
[aka@localhost ~]$ cat ls-output.txt
```

It is important to mention here that some users consider cat being similar to the TYPE command. But the reality is different. Files can be displayed with the help of the cat command without being paged first. The above command displays the contents of ls-output.txt file. The output will come in the form of short text files and not in the form of pages. It speeds up the process. Not only does paging take considerable time, but it is also more complex and time consuming to display it in the form of pages on the screen. You can add multiple files to the cat command as arguments. This command can also be used to append multiple files. If we have multiple files named snazzy.jpeg.01 snazzy.jpeg.02 .... snazzy.jpeg.99

Now you want to join all these files. Let's try the following command.

```
[aka@localhost ~]$ cat snazzy.jpeg.0* > snazzy.jpeg
```

We will have the files in the right order. The cat command welcomes standard input that is linked to our typing something on the keyboard.

```
[aka@localhost ~]$ cat > azure_sky.txt
The sky is turning azure.
```

You have just created a file by using the cat command. You have also put some value in the file. When you are done with the above two steps, press ctrl + d to reach the end of the file. You can bring back the content of the file with the help of the same command.

```
[aka@localhost ~]$ cat azure_sky.txt
the sky is turning azure.
[aka@localhost ~]$
```

Pipelines: Commands can surf through the standard input to read data and then send it to the standard output. This is done with the help of a special shell feature dubbed as pipelines.

```
[aka@localhost ~]$ ls -1 /usr/bin | less
[
ack
addr2line
ag
alias
animalsay
animate
annocheck
appliance-creator
applydeltarpm
appstreamcli
apropos
ar
arch
aria2c
arpaname
as
aserver
aulast
aulastlog
ausyscall
authvar
auvirt
awesome
awesome-client
awk
axel
b2sum
b43-fwcutter
```

This command can be used for a page by page display of what a command sends to the standard output.

Filters: You can utilize pipelines to perform other operations connected to data on your system. You have the freedom to join together multiple commands in a single pipeline which will then be known as *filters*. Let's try one filter. For this one, we are appending together /bin and /usr/bin to see what they have got for us.

```
[aka@localhost ~]# ls /bin /usr/bin | sort | less

[
[
ack
ack
addr2line
addr2line
ag
ag
alias
alias
animalsay
animalsay
animate
animate
annocheck
annocheck
appliance-creator
appliance-creator
applydeltarpm
applydeltarpm
appstreamcli
appstreamcli
apropos
apropos
ar
ar
arch
arch
aria2c
```

44

```
aria2c
arpaname
arpaname
as
as
aserver
aserver
aulast
aulast
aulastlog
aulastlog
ausyscall
ausyscall
authvar
:
[aka@localhost ~]$
```

This is how filters can help you produce a single sorted listed. It is the magic of the *sort* command that we put into the pipeline. Otherwise, there would have been two lists for each directory. It saves times and is more efficient to view multiple directories.

The grep

This also is one of the powerful programs that are used to find text patterns in the files. Let's look at how it is used.

```
[aka@localhost ~]$ grep pattern [file......]
```

This command is used to hunt down matching pattern lines in the files. Let's try out the command.

```
[aka@localhost ~]$ ls /bin /usr/bin | sort | uniq | gre
p zip
```

The head/tail

This command is used to retrieve a specific part of the information. As apparent from the command name, you can print the head or the tail of a particular file. It means you can get the first few lines of a

45

file printed or the last few lines of the same file. Ten lines from the start or ten lines from the last. That's how it goes. The number of lines can be altered by applying the -n option. Let's scroll to the syntax of the command.

```
[aka@localhost ~]$ head -n 8 ls-filename.txt
```

This command can be used in the pipelines as well.

```
[aka@localhost ~]$ ls /usr/bin | tail -n 10
```

With the help of the tail option, you can view the files in real time, and review the progress of the log files while they are in the midst of being written. The following command helps you in reviewing the messages file.

```
[aka@localhost ~]$ tail -f /var/log/messages
```

The option -f is used to monitor real time messages. The command will only show the tail while the messages are being written. They keep popping up on your screen as long as you keep the screen open. To stop it you need to press ctrl + C.

Exploring the tee Command

Linux also has the tee command. Well, you might be thinking of golf at the moment. Just image you are actually in a golf club to tee off. Golf is an amazing sport, but Linux is still better than that when it comes to the thrill and magic of the moment. Another analogy is with plumbing. You have to fix a 't' on a pipe to guide it through your washrooms to the water tank.

This program has a special job of reading the standard input. It reads it and then copies it to the standard output. As a result, the data flows downwards. You can capture what is being passed in the pipeline. Let's see the syntax.

```
[aka@localhost ~]$ ls /usr/bin | tee ls.txt | grep zip
bunzip2
bzip2
bzip2recover
funzip
gunzip
gzip
unzip
unzipsfx
zip
zipcloak
zipgrep
zipinfo
zipnote
zipsplit
[aka@localhost ~]$
```

The *uniq* command

This command is used to sort a file. Both uniq and sort are applied together. To read more about uniq, please take a look at its man page. I have already briefed you about the man page. The following command will not sort the duplicates. You can see by running it on the terminal.

```
[aka@localhost ~]$ ls /bin /usr /bin | sort | uniq -
d | less

[
ack
addr2line
ag
alias
animalsay
animate
annocheck
appliance-creator
applydeltarpm
appstreamcli
apropos
```

```
ar
arch
aria2c
arpaname
as
aserver
aulast
aulastlog
ausyscall
authvar
auvirt
awesome
awesome-client
awk
axel
```

To sort the files you have to remove the -d option from the syntax. Now try it on.

```
[root@localhost ~]$ ls /bin /usr /bin | sort | uniq | l
ess
```

The *wc* Command

As visible from the abbreviation, this one is to count the words in a file content. It also counts how many lines there are in the file content in addition to bytes.

```
[root@localhost ~]$ wc mydocuments.txt
4598   64577   537456      mydocuments.txt
```

It will tell you the number of lines, number of words and total bytes that belong to the mydocuments.txt file. Unlike the Windows operating system, you don't have to search each file content and check out the weight of the file in bytes. The pipeline command will retrieve the information you need.

The Magic of Echo

We know that the echo command displays the text as it is written in the shell. What you don't know is that you can pair up echo with different commands and get marvelous results.

Expansion of some wildcard entries like the (*)

The shell window tends to expand simple commands like the *. While it appears nothing to us users, for the shell it can have lots of meanings. This process is called expansion. The shell interprets such symbols and expands them into words or phrases easy enough to understand. The echo alone is just a print out command. You enter a sentence and the echo prints it out without changing it a bit. Let's see.

```
[aka@localhost ~]$ echo I kept looking at the azure sky
 for five minutes.
I kept looking at the azure sky for five minutes.
[aka@localhost ~]$
```

If we add * after the echo, the result will not be the same. The shell takes * as a wildcard which has a job to match characters in the names of files. It will expand the * into the names of the files that are kept in the directory in which you are working at the moment.

```
[aka@localhost ~]$ echo *
bench.py hello.c
[aka@localhost ~]$
```

The pathname expansion

Let's try something more interesting with the echo command.

```
[aka@localhost ~]$ ls
Desktop ls-output.txt Pictures Templates
Documents Music Public Videos
```

```
[aka@localhost ~]$ echo D*
Desktop Documents
```
and
```
[aka@localhost ~]$ echo *s
Documents Pictures Templates Videos
```

```
[aka@localhost ~]$ echo [[:upper:]]*
```

Desktop Documents Music Pictures Public Templates Videos

Arithmetic expansion: The echo command can also be used to execute arithmetic functions, some quite complex. In this way, the shell prompt does the job of a calculator.

```
[aka@localhost ~]$ echo $((2*2))
4
[aka@localhost ~]$
```

This command can be used for addition, multiplication, subtraction, division, modulo and exponentiation. Either you can do simple mathematics or move on to conduct some complex mathematical operations by nesting different expression in a single script. Let's see how it goes on.

```
[aka@localhost ~]$ echo $(($((5*75))+1000))
1375
```

CHAPTER 3

The Linux Environment

Now that you are well aware of the shell, its usage, and some of the basic commands to execute different tasks, I will move on to the use of kernel. You will get to know how to use the kernel like how it boots and how it starts. Let's take a look at the normal booting process of the kernel. I have divided it into some basic simplified steps.

1. The first step is the BIOS. In this phase, some integrity of the system is thoroughly analyzed. BIOS located the boot loader and executes it. The boot loader can be on a CD, a floppy or a hard drive. After BIOS loads it up on the system, the MBR boot loader has full control. Wondering what is MBR? Let's jump to the next step to understand what MBR is.

2. MBR is the short form of Master Boot Record. MBR can be traced back to the 1st sector of the hard drive or any other bootable disk. The sector in the hard drive is titled as /dev/had or /dev/sda. MBR is a very light program when it comes to size. Its major component is the primary boot loader which is just shy of 512 bytes. This information in the form of a few bytes is mainly about GRUB. Sylvia learned it in a chain like system like BIOS loads the MBR then MBR load the GRUB.

3. What is GRUB ? It is the short form of Grand Unified Bootloader. GRUB also is a loader for kernel images. If you there is one kernel image on your system, GRUB will take it as the default image and loads it right away. If there are multiple images, GRUB will bring out a splash screen that has multiple images. You have got to choose one for loading. If you don't go for one, GRUB will load the default image as per settings in the configuration file.

4. The fourth step is the kernel itself. Kernel runs the */sbin/init* program which has 1 as the process id. The term *init* can be expanded to *initrd* that can be further expanded into initial RAM Disk. Kernel uses it for a short window of time from being booted to mounting of root file system.

5. After *init* starts running, you reach the *user space start*. The *init* takes over from there by running the system.

The Startup

A wide range of diagnostic messages are produced at the booting time originating from the kernel in the start then from the processes after *init* takes over the operations of the system. The messages don't run in a sequence and also, they are not consistent. For a new user, they can be confusing and even misleading. Some of the Linux distribution mechanisms try to slash them with the help of splash screens and changes in boot options. You can see and read these messages by the following commands. Let's see. I have logged in as a superuser. Let's look at the result of the command.

```
[aka@localhost ~]$ dmesg

[    0.000000] OF: fdt: Ignoring memory range 0x8000000
0 - 0x80200000

[    0.000000] Linux version 4.15.0-00049-ga3b1e7a-
dirty (bellard@localhost.loca
```

ldomain) (gcc version 7.3.0 (Buildroot 2016.08-git-svn30683)) #11 Thu Nov 8 20:3

0:26 CET 2018

It makes use of the ring buffer of the kernel. The above is a short version of what you will see on the page. It may not be exactly the same as above, but it will be nearly the same. Let's explore the dmesg command with different options to get more information.

```
[aka@localhost ~]$ dmesg | less
```

You can use other options with the *dmesg* command. Let's take a look at different options that can be explored in Linux. I will not go into the details of what you will see on your screens. But I will definitely tell you what can you expect by entering each command. Let's see the syntax. This time I have switched the user.

```
[aka@localhost ~]$ dmesg -C        You can use this
command to clear the kernel ring buffer
[aka@localhost ~]$ dmesg -c        You can apply this
command to clear all the messages.
[aka@localhost ~]$ dmesg -k        This is used to
read kernel messages.
[aka@localhost ~]$ dmesg -L        It colorizes the
content of messages.
```

Other options are the following. Enter them in the terminal and see what they may bring to you.

```
 [aka@localhost ~]$ dmesg -D
[aka@localhost ~]$ dmesg -r
[aka@localhost ~]$ dmesg -s
[aka@localhost ~]$ dmesg -n
[aka@localhost ~]$ dmesg -F
[aka@localhost ~]$ dmesg -e
```

What Boot Options Do You have When Kernel Initializes

Kernel initialization in Linux consists of some key steps. It starts with the examination of the Central Processing Unit (CPU). After that, memory is examined. Then comes the device is discovered, root filesystem goes operational and in the end user space starts.

The Parameters: When the kernel starts running, it receives its *parameters* from the boot loader. These parameters guide the kernel on how should it start. These parameters carry specifications on the diagnostic output, as well as options, on the drivers of the device. The parameters can be viewed by a dedicated command. Let's look at the syntax.

```
[aka@localhost ~]$ cat /proc/cmdline
```

Not all parameters are important but one which is the root parameter. The kernel is unable to operate without it because it just cannot locate *init*. You might be thinking of adding something in the parameter that it doesn't understand? Well, Sylvia added it for sure. She added the -s in the parameters. The kernel saved the unknown phrase and moved it to *init*. The kernel interprets it as the command to start in the single user mode.

The bootloaders: A bootloader is a program that is responsible for loading the tasks necessary for at the boot time. Additionally, it loads the operating system. In the world of technology, a bootloader is also called boot manager. As I have already explained, this program is kickstarted after the BIOS are done with performing the initial checks on hardware. Now we know that the kernel and parameters lie on root filesystem.

Let's take a brief look at what is the job of a bootloader.

A bootloader has to select one kernel from multiple options. Secondly, with the aid of a bootloader, users can manually override names of kernel images, as well as parameters. It also allows you to switch between different kernel parameters.

Bootloaders are now not the same as before. They have become more advanced with added features like the option of history, as well as menu. However, experts still believe that the basic job of the bootloader is to offer different options regarding the kernel image as well as selection of parameters.

Let's take a look at multiple bootloaders that you may come across when you enter the field. GRUB, LOADLIN, LILO, coreboot are some of the most popular bootloaders of this age. Let's explore GRUB.

Getting into the Details of GRUB

Bootloaders are one of the reasons due to which users run away from Linux operating systems. If you are Windows OS user, you don't have to bother about the bootloader, but this is not the case with Linux operating system. As a Windows user, you switch on the laptop or your personal computer and that's it. If there is a problem in the booting system, you can simply run the Windows Recovery program to repair the damage and bring the operating system to its normal health. You just have to click on the button and the rest is the job of the operating system itself. That's quite amazing, but the biggest problem with it is that you cannot learn anything about the insides of the operating system. Sylvia had been a Windows user for ten years and she didn't have the faintest idea about what a bootloader is, what is its job, and how can you use it?

Linux takes the tough course. It makes users learn the intricate details about complex things in the operating system. It reroutes our minds toward the background technology of the operating system. Let's move on to the bootloader itself to understand how it processes. So, how does it work?

You make your computer boot and as I have explained, the BIOS, after running some checks, passes the control of the machine to the boot device that differs from user to user. It can be a floppy or a hard disk drive. We already know that the hard disk has different sectors. The first of which is known as Master Boot Record (MBR).

GRUB drives out the MBR code and fills in its own. It helps users navigate the file system, which facilitates users to select the desired kernel image as well as configuration. GRUB is the short form of *Grand Unified Boot Loader*. Just explore the menu of the GRUB to learn more about it. Mostly the bootloader is hidden from the users and in order to access the bootloader, you should hold the SHIFT button for a while immediately after the BIOS startup shows up. There also is an automatic reboot problem. To avoid that, press ESC and disable the timeout of automatic reboot which starts counting right after the GRUB menu shows up. If you want to view the configuration commands of the boot loader, press e to enter the default boot option.

Getting familiarized with GRUB

Let's get to know the GRUB notation. Let's take a look at the GRUB entry.

```
(hd0,1)
```

If you look at the entry, you will know that the brackets are an integral part of the entry. You remove them, you disturb the syntax. All the devices in GRUB have brackets on them. The hd means hard disk. If the device is other than the hard disk, the value will be replaced with fd (floppy disk) and cd for CD-ROM. Please note that there also are two numbers. The first number refers to the number of the hard drive in the system. Here it denotes the first hard drive. Similarly, 1 denotes the second hard drive while 2 denotes the third har drive. That's how it goes on.

You can change the value of the integers by putting in the number of the hard disk that you want to explore. It is evident from the entry that GRUB cannot differentiate between different types of drives like SCSI and IDE. In the GRUB menu the primary partitions can be identified from integers from 0 to 3 where 0 is for the first hard disk while 3 is for the fourth partition. Logical partitions move from 4 to upwards.

GRUB can search all partitions for a UUID to locate the kernel. If you want to see how the GRUB works on the Linux operating system, just hit C while you are at the editor and you will reach the GRUB prompt. Something similar to the following will appear on the screen of the editor.

```
grub>
```

This is the GRUB command line. Get started by entering any command here. In order to get started, you need to run a diagnostic command.

```
grub> ls
(hd0) (h0,msdos1)
```

The result will be a list of devices that are already known to the GRUB. You can see that there is just one disk, the hd0, and one partition, (hd0,msdos1). The information we can get from this is that the disk contains an MBR partition table.

To delve deeper into more information, enter ls -l on the GRUB command line.

```
grub> ls -l
```

This command tells us more about the partitions on the disk.

You can easily navigate files on the GRUB system. Let's take a look at its filesystem navigation. First of all, you need to find out about the GRUB root.

```
grub> echo $root
hd0,msdos1
```

You should use the ls command in order to list the files as well as directories in the root. Let's see how to do that.

```
grub> ls ($root)/
```

You may expect a list of directory names that are on that particular partition. The filesystem and the directories can eb listed in the form of *etc/,bin/,* and *dev/.*

How to Configure GRUB

The configuration directory has the central file titled *grub.cfg*. In addition, these multiple modules that are loaded on the system are also part of the configuration system. These modules are named as *.mod*. This should be the beginning of the configuration system.

```
### BEGIN /etc/grub.d/00_header ###
```

All the files in the directory /etc/grub.d are multiple shell script programs. By combining they make up the central configuration file that is grub.cfg. This is the default shape of the GRUB configuration. Now let's move on to the function which allows you to alter the command. The short answer is that you can do that easily. You can customize it according to your needs. You know that a central file for configuration exists. You just have to create another file for customization purposes. You can name the file as *customized.cfg*. This will be added to the configuration directory of GRUB. You can find it following this path: */boot/grub/custom.cfg.*

There are two options concerning customization. The directory of configuration can be accessed at /etc/grub.d. This directory offers 40_customa and 41_custom. 40_custom can be edited on your own without any aid, but it is prone to be weak and unstable. The other one that is 41_custom is much simple than the previous one. This file contains a string of commands ready to be loaded when the GRUB starts. A small example is that Ubuntu, a Linux distribution network, allows users to edit the configuration settings by adding memory tester options (memtest86+).

If you want to write a fresh configuration and also want to install it on the system, you can do that by writing the configuration to the directory with the help of using the -0 option. Let's see the syntax to conclude the configuration process.

```
# grub-mkconfig -o /boot/grub/grub.cfg.
```

For users of the Ubuntu Linux distribution system, things are pretty much simple and easy. All you need is to run the following command.

```
install-grub
```

How to Install GRUB

Before you move on to the installer, please read what this bootloader requires for installation purpose. Please determine the following.

- GRUB directory, as seen by the current system, should be properly analyzed. /boot/grub is the directory's name usually. The name can be something else if you are installing GRUB on another system.

- You have to determine what device the GRUB target disk is using.

As GRUB is a modular system, it needs to read the filesystem which is contained in the GRUB directory.

```
#grub-install /dev/sda
```

In this command, grub-install is the command used to install the GRUB, and /dev/sda is the current hard disk that I am using.

59

If you do it wrong, that can cause many problems for you because of its power to alter the bootup sequence on the system. This increase the importance of this command. You need to have an emergency bootup plan if something actually goes wrong along the way.

Install GRUB on an External Device

You can also install GRUB on an external device. You have to specify the directory first on which it will install. For example, if you have */dev/sda* on your system. Your system will see the GRUB files in */mnt/boot/grub*. You have to guide the system by entering the following command.

```
# grub-install –boot-directory=/mnt/boot /dev/sda
```

Let's see how GRUB works

It consists of multiple steps. Let's take them on one by one.

- We now know the drill of how the Linux operating system starts. BIOS kicks off in the start. When it has run necessary checks on the device, it initializes the device's hardware. After that, it tries to trace out the boot-order in order to get the boot code.

- When it has found the boot code, the next step is the loading of BIOS or the firmware. Then comes its execution. After that is the time for the start of GRUB.

- GRUB starts to load on your Linux operating system.

- First of all, the core kickstarts. Now GRUB is in a better position to access your hard disks and the filesystems that you have stored on the system.

- Then GRUB moves on to identify the partition from which it has to boot. Next step is to load the configuration.

- Now, as a user, this is the time when you have the power to alter the configuration if you need it to be.

- If you don't want to alter it, the timeout will end shortly. Now GRUB will execute the default or altered configuration.

- While trying to execute the configuration, GRUB loads some additional code in the form of modules in the partition from which it has booted.

- Now GRUB runs the boot command and execute the kernel.

I share my weekend routine with Sylvia. I am an enthusiast of outdoor activities like hunting by a crossbow out in the wild. Sylvia likes cycling in rough and hilly terrains. We really enjoy when we are together on the weekends. It was rare for her to miss a weekend. But finally, she missed it not one but three in a row. So, I phoned her to know what was the matter. To which she responded that her limited knowledge of Linux was not helping her at the office. She was worried because she was highly pressed for wrapping up her work while most of the time struggled with the learning process. This time it was the user space and the environment. Though it is not that difficult to learn, it takes time before you get used to it

Not that much time, I must admit, that Sylvia has consumed. With the right guidance, you can move through it like a pro. The more you practice the better understanding you will have on it. User space refers to the point where the kernel starts. How the user space moves on. Let's see in the following steps.

- init

- low level services start like udevd as well as syslogd

- The network is configured.

- Services like printing go on.

- Next come the login shells, the Graphical User Interface (GUI).

- Other apps start running that you might have installed on the Linux operating system.

The init

This is a user space program which can be located in the /sbin directory. You can locate the directory if you run the PATH command. PATH is a variable. I'll discuss this variable in-depth in the upcoming chapters. System V init, Upstart and System V init are implementations of init in its Linux distributions. Android has its own unique *init*.

System V init triggered a sequence that required just one task while the system starts up. This system appears easy, but seriously hampers the performance of the kernel. In addition, advanced users abhor this kind of simplified startup. The system starts up following a fixed set of services, so if you want any new service to run on the system, no standardized way is available here in order to accommodate any new components. So that's a minus.

On the other hand, Upstart as well as systemd rectify the performance issue. They accommodate several services to take a start in parallel to pace up the boot. The systemd is for the people who are looking out for a goal-oriented system. You will have the flexibility of defining your target and the time span you need to achieve the target. In addition, it resolves the target. Another attractive option is that you can delay the start of a particular service until you want it to load.

Upstart receives different events and runs different tasks that result in the production of more events. Consequently, Upstart runs more jobs. As a user, you can get an advanced way to track services. These latest *init* systems are free of scripts.

Runlevels in Linux

When you boot a Linux operating system, it moves into the default runlevel and also tends to run the scripts that are attached to the specific runlevel. Runlevels are of different types and you can also switch between them off and on. To quote an example, there is a runlevel specifically designed for system recovery and tasks related to maintenance of the operating system. As an example, System V init scripts are used as default runlevel. Ubuntu uses the same.

We are well aware of the fact by now that *init*, that is launched by Linux in the start, in turn, launches other system processes. If you want to control what *init* should launch and what not, you should edit the startup script which the *init* reads. An interesting thing about *init* is that it has the ability to run different runlevels like one for networking, another for the graphical user interface. Switching between the runlevels is also easy. All it takes is a single command to jump from the graphical desktop to the text console. It saves lots of time. Let's move further into the runlevels to understand them better.

System V Runlevels

There are different sets of processes running in the system like *crond*. These runlevels are categorized from 0 to 6. A system starts with a specific runlevel but shuts down using another runlevel that has a particular set of script in order to properly close all the programs in a proper way and also to stop the kernel. If you have a Linux system in place you can enter the following command and check in which runlevel you are at the moment.

```
[aka@localhost ~]$ who -r
```

Your screen will tell you the stage of your runlevel on a scale from 0 to 6, and also the date and time at which the runlevel was created on the system. Runlevels in the Linux operating system has many jobs to do, such as differentiating among shutdown, the startup, the text console mode and the different user modes. The seven numbers from 0 to 6 can be allocated to different channels. Linux operating systems that are based on Fedora allocate 5 to the graphical user interface and 4 to the text console.

In a standard runlevel o is allocated to shutting down of the system, 6 is allocated to the reboot while 1 is allocated to the single user mode.

I know you are finding these runlevels quite interesting, but they are now going obsolete.

system init

The system init can help you in better handling of the system bootup and also aids you in handling services like *cron* and *inetd*. One feature that users love it is its ability to delay the start of operating system and other services until they are imperative. The full form of systemd is System Management Daemon. The *systemd* is now replacing *init*, and there are some pretty solid reasons behind this shakeup. Let's see how *init* starts the system.

One task starts when the last startup returns successful and gets loaded up on the memory of the operating system. This causes undue delay in the booting time of the system, which resulted in frustration for the users. Now it is quite logical to think that system adds some fuel to speed up the process, but sorry you are wrong. Well, it does decrease the booting time, not by putting in some extra gas, but by removing the speed breakers, like finishing the necessary tasks neatly.

It does so much on your system that its responsibilities are somewhat difficult to grasp in a single discussion, but I'll try my best. Let's see what it does on your system.

- It improves efficiency by properly ordering the tasks, which makes the booting process simpler.

- It loads up the configuration of your system.

- The default boot goal, along with its dependencies, is determined.

- Boot goal is activated.

The difference between *systemd* and *init* is the flexibility which the former has to offer to the user. The *systemd* just avoids unnecessary startup sequences.

The Linux Environment

It was the fall. Yellowish red leaves were falling from the trees like the angels who were banished from the heavens. Pale and defeated, they rested on the pathway and the greenbelt along the road. An old woman with a cane in hand was trying to cross the road. Luckily, she got help from a young blondie lady who happened to be passing by. It was Sunday. The sun was far into the thick clouds that were hovering over the city's skyscrapers, but it was balmy, the kind of weather you like to visit a beach. To the beach did I go. But wait a minute. Did I say something about the young blondie lady who was helping the lady? Oooops! That's Sylvia. And yes, she did accompany me to the beach.

"Lovely weather today? Mind a drink?" and she pulled out a bottle of peach pulp. "I don't mind that." I replied with a smile. "Well, well, well, finally I have started getting acquainted myself with Linux," she started. I stared at her with a little frown that wasn't matured yet on my face. "For God sake. We are on the weekend. If by a stroke of the ill fate, you have joined me on this beach, please don't spoil the moment." But she was unstoppable as are with newbie learners of Linux and programming languages.

I gave in. She was curious about the Linux environment on that particular day. Well, the subject was a juicy one, so I went on trying to educate her more about it. By imaging about the environment of Linux, and the beach where I was out sunbathing, the image before your eyes might be something interesting. Perhaps your brain is trying to structure an analogy between the environment for Linux and the general environment that surrounds us.

Let me explain. Yes, it is more or less the same. Just like we live in the environment; the shell window is also surrounded by an environment of its own. Whatever data that you store in the Linux environment is accessible to programs for the determination of facts about the configuration of the system. It is pertinent here to mention that the environment can be used to customize the shell experience. You can find the environment and shell variables in the environment. We will be using two commands to examine the environment; the set command and the printenv command. The latter command shows only the environment variables. I will not expand it here as you are going to see lots of it in the next chapter. So, let's run the set command. In order to do away with a long list of variables and other info, I'll pipe the output by pairing up the set command with the less command.

```
[aka@localhost ~]$ set | less
BASH=/bin/sh
BASHOPTS=checkwinsize:cmdhist:complete_fullquote:expand
_aliases:extquote:force_f
ignore:histappend:hostcomplete:interactive_comments:log
in_shell:progcomp:promptv
ars:sourcepath
BASHRCSOURCED=Y
BASH_ALIASES=()
BASH_ARGC=()
BASH_ARGV=()
BASH_CMDS=()
BASH_LINENO=()
BASH_SOURCE=()
```

```
BASH_VERSINFO=([0]="4" [1]="4" [2]="23" [3]="1" [4]="re
lease" [5]="riscv64-koji-
linux-gnu")
BASH_VERSION='4.4.23(1)-release'
COLUMNS=80
CVS_RSH=ssh
DIRSTACK=()
EUID=0
GROUPS=()
HISTCONTROL=ignoredups
HISTFILE=/root/.bash_history
HISTFILESIZE=1000
HISTSIZE=1000
HOME=/root
HOSTNAME=localhost
HOSTTYPE=riscv64
IFS='
'
'
LANG=en_US.UTF-8
[aka@localhost ~]$
```

The set command distinguishes itself from the rest of the lot by displaying the information in a near alphabetical order which is quite user-friendly. In addition, to that you can use the echo command to pull out information on the variable you need.

```
[aka@localhost ~]$ echo $HOSTNAME
localhost
[aka@localhost ~]$ echo $HOSTTYPE
riscv64
[aka@localhost ~]$ echo $HOME
/root
```

Moving on with the exploration of the shell environment I'll test the alias command.

```
[root@localhost ~]$ alias
egrep='egrep --color=auto'
fgrep='fgrep --color=auto'
grep='grep --color=auto'
```

```
l.='ls -d .* --color=auto'
ll='ls -l --color=auto'
ls='ls --color=auto'
mc='. /usr/libexec/mc/mc-wrapper.sh'
which='(alias; declare -f) | /usr/bin/which --tty-
only --read-alias --read-funct
ions --show-tilde --show-dot'
xzegrep='xzegrep --color=auto'
xzfgrep='xzfgrep --color=auto'
xzgrep='xzgrep --color=auto'
zegrep='zegrep --color=auto'
zfgrep='zfgrep --color=auto'
zgrep='zgrep --color=auto'
[aka@localhost ~]$
```

Some of the other important variables include HOME, LANG, SHELL, DISPLAY, PAGER and OLD_PWD. Each has its own function like HOME leads you to the pathname of the home directory. EDITOR tells you about what kind of program you are using to edit the shell scripts. Similarly, DISPLAY shows the name of the display just in case you are running a graphical environment.

Some additional variables that are interesting as well as very handy are TZ which is used to specify the timezone, USER which tells your username, PS1 which explores the contents of the shell, and the PWD which explores the directory in which you are currently working.

CHAPTER 4

Package Management & Storage on Linux Systems

W hen it comes to Linux distribution, most newbie or casual users are more concerned about the color schemes and different other unnecessary features when selecting which distribution best suits them. What they forget to take into consideration is the fact that the most important thing is the packaging system of Linux in combination with the support community of each distribution system. We know it is open source. The software is dynamic and not static like the Windows. It just keeps on changing by contributions from the community members.

With the help of package management, we can install and maintain software on our personal computer systems. The following section will tell you about the tools to deals with package management. All these tools are linked to the command line. Some people may question if Linux distributors offer a graphical user interface why should we be forced into the command line yet again. The answer is simple. Command line tools offer us the completion of some impossible tools that the graphical user interface find impossible to conclude.

The Packaging System

The packaging systems differ from various distribution systems, and they are also distribution specific. You cannot use one packaging system on multiple distributions. In general, there are two main packaging systems:

- The Debian (.deb)

- The Red Hat (.rmp)

Most Linux distributions fall under these two main camps, but the packaging system is not limited to the two. There are some important exceptions, like Slackware and Gentoo.

Ubuntu, Linspire and Debian use the (.deb) camp. Mandriva, Fedora, Red Hat Enterprise Linux, and PCLinuxOS use the (.rpm) camp.

How it Works

Usually software is bought from the market and then installed from a disk. You run the installation wizard and get the app on your system. This is a standard process on a Windows system. Linux is different. You don't have to buy anything as almost all software can be found on the web space for free. The distribution vendors offer the code compiled and stuffed in package files or they put it as source code which you have to install manually. The latter demands pro-level skills.

A package file can be dubbed as the basic unit of Linux software. It can be further explored into sets of files that together make up the software package. A bigger question is, what does a package have? It has multiple programs in addition to including metadata which shows the text description of the file as well as the contents. There are package maintainers who create the package files. These package maintainers can be but not always are employees of the vendors who distribute the Linux system. The package maintainers receive the source code for the software and produces the metadata and installation scripts. They can opt to contribute to the source code or leave it as it is received.

Repositories

The distribution vendors do most of the work related to creating these packages. When they have been prepared, vendors or any third parties who created them place them in the central repositories. The central repositories are like mines of package files. The package files in the repositories are specifically created for the distribution.

There can be more than one repository in a Linux distribution. Let's take a look at a few:

- Testing repository: this repository is filled with packages that are usually used by skilled Linux users who are looking forward to testing bugs in the packages before they reach a common user.

- Development repository: another repository is the development repository, which contains the packages under development and will soon be included in the next release by the distribution.

- Third party repository: well, that's what it is called. This repository contains packages that are created by third parties but cannot be made a part of the distribution's major releases out of legal bars. Countries that have pretty relaxed laws related to software patents allow the third-party repositories to be released by Linux distribution. Although they can be included in the distribution's release, yet they are not part of the distribution and must be included manually in the configuration files.

The Dependencies

Linux programs need support from several software components to work efficiently. Some packages demand a shared source to get the work done. This shared source, such as a shared library, is dubbed as the dependency for the package file. Therefore, most of the Linux distribution systems also contain their dependencies in the package so that the software functions smoothly.

The tools to manage packages

There usually are two types of tools for package management:

- The low-end tools are used to tackle basic tasks like installation and uninstallation of package files on the system.

- The high-end tools are used to conduct meta-data search and resolve the dependency problem.

Let's take a look at some common tools that come with Linux distribution systems.

Low-end tools

The dpkg is considered as a low-end tool for the Debian style while rpm is a low-end tool for Red Hat Enterprise, CentOS and Fedora.

High-end tools

The aptitude and apt-get are some high-end tools for the Debian style while yum is considered as a high-end tool for Red Hat Enterprise, CentOS and Fedora.

You can use these tools to wrap up different key tasks, such as locating a particular package from the repositories.

You can install a package

You can use the following commands to install a package in the Debian style.

- *apt-get install package_name*

- *apt-get update*

For Red Hat style, use the following command.

- *yum install package_name*

Also, you can install a package right from a particular package file. Let's see how to do that. This is for the package files that are not part of a repository and are installed directly. Let's see the commands:

For the users of the Debian style, the following command is used.

- *dpkg –install package_file*

For the users of the Red Hat style, the following command is used.

- rpm -i package_file

You can also delete a particular package from the system by using these simple tools. Let's take a look at the commands

For the Debian style users, the following command tool is the best.

- *Apt-get remove package-name*

For the Red Hat style users, the following command tool works well.

- *yum erase package-name*

You can do more with the help of command tools. Suppose you have installed a package system and now you want to update it. You can do that with the following tools. As with the above-mentioned tasks, the tools for the Debian and the Red Hat were different, the same is the case with the updating tools.

- For the Debian style users, the command tool for updating the package system is *apt-get update*. You can also replace *update* with *upgrade*. Both do the same job.

- The Red Hate style users can with the command *yum update*.

If you have downloaded an updated version of a package from a non-repository source, you can install it by replacing the previous version. The commands for the job are as under:

- The Debian style users should enter *dpkg –install package-file*.

- The Red Hat style users should enter *rpm -U package-file*.

Replace package-file with the name of the file that you want to update. When you have installed more than one packages over a particular course of time, and you want to view them in the form of a list, you can use the following tool to see the record.

- For the Debian style users *dpkg --list* is the tool to view the list.

- For the Red Hat style users *rpm -qa* should be entered.

When you have installed a package, you check its status any time to make sure it is there on your Linux operating system. There are some handy tools available for the purpose. Let's check out.

- The Debian style users should enter type *dpkg --status package-name*.

- The Red Hat style users may use *rpm -q package-name*.

In addition to checking the status of an installed package, you also can explore more information about it with the help of the following commands.

- The Debian style users may enter *apt-cache show package-name.*

- The Red Hat style users can type *yum info package-name.*

Storage Media

We know about hard disk drives, floppy disks, and CD drives from the Windows operating system. If you think Windows makes it easy for you to handle them, Linux has more to offer. You can handle all the storage devices like the hard disk drive, the virtual storage such as the RAID, the network storage, and Logical Volume Manager (LVM). I'll explain some key commands that you can use to handle all the storage devices easily as well as efficiently.

The commands for mounting and dismounting storage devices

You can mount and dismount a storage device with the help of some simple commands. If you are using a non-desktop system, you will have to do that manually owing to the fact that servers have some complex requirements for system configuration.

There are some steps involved to accomplish the objective like linking the storage device with the filesystem tree. Programmers call it mounting. After this, you the storage device starts participating in the functions of the operating system. We have already learned about the filesystem tree earlier on. All the storage devices are connected to the filesystem tree. This is where it differs from the Windows system, which has separate trees for each device. As an example, see the C:\ and D:\ drives. You can explore the list of the devices with the help of the command */etc/fstab.*

If you want to view the list of the filesystems that you already have mounted on the Linux computer system. We call it the mount command. By entering it on the command line, you will get the list of the mounted filesystems.

```
[aka@localhost ~]$ mount
```

The listing will show the mount-point type as well as the filesystem-type.

You can determine names of the devices

Although determining names of the devices is considered as a difficult task to do, yet there are some easy ways to master it. To make out the names of the devices, we have to first list the devices on the Linux operating system.

```
[aka@localhost ~]$ ls /dev
```

Let's analyze the names of different devices.

/dev/hd* *:* These are PATA disks on the older systems. The typical motherboards have a couple of IDE connectors. Each of the IDEs had a cable and a couple of points for drives to get attached to them. The first drive is dubbed as the master drive while the other one is named as the slave drive. You can find them by referring them as /dev/hda for the master drive and as /dev/hdb for the slave drive. These names are given to the drives in the first channel. For the second channel, you can refer the master drive as /dev/hdc and the list goes on. If you see a digit at the end of the titles, remember that it refers to the partition. To quote an example, /dev/hda1 will be considered as the 1st partition to on the first hard drive. In this scenario where you have partitions, the name /dev/had will refer to the full drive.

/dev/fd*: This name refers to the floppy disk drives.

/dev/sd*: This refers to the SCSI disks, which includes all PATA and SATA hard disk drives, the flash drives, the USB mass storage drives like the portable music players and the ports to connect digital cameras.

How to create new filesystems?

On Linux, you have the freedom to create new filesystems. Suppose you want to reformat the flash drive with the help of a Linux native filesystem instead of the FAT32 system. You can do that by following two simple steps, such as the following:

- You can create a fresh layout for a new partition if you don't like the current partition.

- Secondly, you can create a new, but empty, filesystem.

This command will format your current hard disk partitions so remember to use it on a spare disk and not on the one that stores your important data. A single mistake in the name of the drive can result in erasing data on the wrong drive.

You can use the *fdisk* program to interact with the hard disk drive and other flash drives on your Linux computer system. The *fdisk* program allows you to edit, create or delete partitions on one particular device. In this case, I'll be dealing with the flash drive.

```
[aka@localhost ~]$ sudo umount /dev/sdb1
[aka@localhost ~]$ sudo fdisk /dev/sdb
```

The first command will unmount the flash drive and with the second command you can invoke the *fdisk* program. The following will appear on the screen.

```
Command (m for help):
```

When you see that on the screen, enter 'm' on the keyboard which will display a menu that will prompt a command action from the user. By pressing *b,* you can edit the disk. By pressing *d,* you can delete a particular partition of the device. In this particular case, we are into the flash drive so the *d* key will delete a partition from the flash drive. You can press *l* to list the partitions that are not yet known. You can print the menu again any time by pressing *m*. Also, you can add a new partition to the device by pressing *n*. By pressing *q*, you can quit the menu without saving the necessary changes and by pressing *t*, you can change the system id of a partition.

First of all, you are required to see the layout for a particular partition. Press *p* to see the partition table for the flash drive device.

Now suppose we have a dummy storage device of 32 MB having one partition, and this device can be identified as Windows 95 FAT32. From the menu, you can see that there is an option for listing the known partition types when you press *l*. Now you can see all the possible types. It is pertinent to mention here that the b in the *sdb* refers to the partition id. In the list, you can recognize your partition with the help of the system id '*b*'. You can change the system id for your particular partition by entering *t* on the command line. The changes have been stored on the system until now. Remember that you have not touched the device as of now. Now enter *w* to modify the partition table to the device and make an exit. You have successfully altered the partition. If at any time you decide to leave the partition without altering it, press *q* and exit the command line.

Now that you have learned to edit the flash drive device partition, we should move on to create a new filesystem with the help of *mkfs* command. Read it as make filesystem. An interesting thing is that you can create filesystems in multiple formats.

If you want to create ext3, add -t option to the command mkfs. Let's see the syntax for the command.

```
[aka@localhost ~]$ sudo mkfs -t ext3 /dev/sdb1
```

There will be plenty of information displayed on your screen. You can get back to the other types by the following commands. To reformat the device to the FAT32 filesystem, you can draft the following command and enter on the command line.

```
[aka@localhost ~]$ sudo mkfs -t /dev/sdb1
```

You can see that editing a partition, formatting it, and creating a new filesystem are pretty easy on the Linux operating system than that of the Windows system. You can repeat the following the above-mentioned simple steps whenever you want to add a new device to your computer system. This kind of freedom of altering the type of a storage device and editing it is unavailable in the Windows operating system. In the above example, I described the entire process with the help of a dummy flash drive. You have the liberty to practice the above commands on a hard disk drive or any other removable storage. Whatever suits you, you can go for it.

CHAPTER 5

Linux Environment Variables

When talking about the bash shell, it is relevant to know about its features like the environment variables. These variables come handy in storing information about a particular shell session as well as the environment in which you have been working. With the help of these variables, you can feed information in the memory which can be accessed through running a script or simply by running a program.

Global Variables

This is simple to learn. These are the variables that can be accessed globally. In simple words, you can access them at any phase of the program. When you have declared a variable, it is fed into the memory of the system while you run the program. You can offer alterations in any function that may affect the entire program. Global variables are always displayed in capital letters.

```
[aka@localhost ~]$ printenv
```

You have had a full list of global environment variables. Most of them are set during the login process. If you want to track down values of individual variables, you can do that with the help of *echo* command. Just don't forget to add the $ sign before the variable to get its value. Let's look at the syntax.

```
[aka@localhost ~]$ echo $PWD
/root
[aka@localhost ~]$
```

Local Environment Variables

These can only be seen in the local process. Both global environment variables and local environment variables are equally valuable. It is difficult to get a list of the local environment variables because you can't just run a single command for the purpose. The set command shows the environment variables set for a particular purpose.

```
[aka@localhost ~]$ set
BASH=/bin/bash
BASHOPTS=checkwinsize:cmdhist:complete_fullquote:expand
_aliases:extquote:force_f
ignore:histappend:hostcomplete:interactive_comments:pro
gcomp:promptvars:sourcepa
th
BASHRCSOURCED=Y
BASH_ALIASES=()
BASH_ARGC=()
BASH_ARGV=()
BASH_CMDS=()
BASH_LINENO=()
BASH_SOURCE=()
BASH_VERSINFO=([0]="4" [1]="4" [2]="23" [3]="1" [4]="re
lease" [5]="riscv64-koji-
linux-gnu")
BASH_VERSION='4.4.23(1)-release'
COLUMNS=80
CVS_RSH=ssh
DIRSTACK=()
EUID=0
GROUPS=()
HISTCONTROL=ignoredups
HISTFILE=/root/.bash_history
HISTFILESIZE=1000
HISTSIZE=1000
HOME=/root
```

```
HOSTNAME=localhost
HOSTTYPE=riscv64
IFS=$' \t\n'
LANG=en_US.UTF-8
LESSOPEN='||/usr/bin/lesspipe.sh %s'
LINES=30
```

Please take into account the fact that all the global variables also are included in the *set* command details.

You can set your own local environment variables

You can set your own variables in the bash shell. You can assign value to a variable by using the equal sign.

```
[aka@localhost ~]$ test=world
[aka@localhost ~]$ echo $test
world
[aka@localhost ~]$
```

The above example is fit for assigning simple values. In order to assign a string value with spaces between words, you need to try something different. Please note that you have to use lower case letters in order to create a new variable. This is important because you can get confused by seeing the environment variables in the capital case. Let's take a look at the following syntax:

```
[aka@localhost ~]$ test=theskyisazure
[aka@localhost ~]$ echo $test
theskyisazure
[aka@localhost ~]$ test=the sky is azure
bash: sky: command not found
[aka@localhost ~]$ test='the sky is azure'
[aka@localhost ~]$ echo $test
the sky is azure
```

You can see that the difference lies in the use of single quotation marks.

82

How to remove environment variables

You can remove the variables with a simple step. Let's see the syntax of the *unset* command.

```
[aka@localhost ~]$ echo $test
theskyisazure
[aka@localhost ~]$ unset test
[aka@localhost ~]$ echo $ test
[aka@localhost ~]$
```

If you remove the environment variable from the child process, it still remains in the parent process. You have to remove it from the parent process separately.

```
[aka@localhost ~]$ test=azure
[aka@localhost ~]$ export test
[aka@localhost ~]$ bash
[aka@localhost ~]$ echo $test
azure
[aka@localhost ~]$ unset test
[aka@localhost ~]$ echo $test

[aka@localhost ~]$ $exit
[aka@localhost ~]$ echo $test
azure
[aka@localhost ~]$
```

You can clearly see that the environment variable was first exported so that it may become a global variable. The unset command was applied while I was still in the child process. When I switched to the parent shell, the command was still valid. That's why you need to delete it from the parent shell as well.

Check out the default shell variables

The bash shell contains environment variables that originate from the shell itself. Let's check out some of the variables.

```
[aka@localhost ~]$ echo $PATH
```

```
/usr/local/sbin:/bin:/sbin:/usr/bin:/usr/sbin:/usr/loca
l/bin
```

You can see different directories in this command. The shell looks for commands in these directories. More directories can be added to the command just by inserting colon and then adding the directory. A default value is assigned to the variables. Let's take a look at the following table.

PATH   As I have shown you by an example, it carries the list of the directories.
HOME   This refers to the home directory of the user.
IFS   This brings out a list of characters
CDPATH   You will get a list of directories that are separated by a colon.

Importance of the PATH Variable

This is perhaps the most important variable in the Linux system because it guides the shell to locate the commands for execution right after you enter on the command line. In case it fails to locate it, an error message will be displayed which can look similar to the one given as under:

```
[aka@localhost ~]$ newfile
-bash : newfile: command not found
[aka@localhost ~]$
```

It is an environmental variable in the Linux operating system. It becomes active as you enter a command or a shell script. A shell script is just like a mini program that offers text-only user interface for the users of Unix-like systems. It can read commands and then execute them accordingly. It is important to consider here that PATH with all capitals must not be replaced with a path with all the lower-case letters.

84

The path variable is a completely different thing as it is the address of a directory. Relative path alludes to the address in relation to the directory you are currently in. There also is an absolute path as already discussed, which is the address in relation to the root directory.

On the other hand, the PATH will turn out a series of paths distinguished by colons and stored in the form of plain text files. For revision and explanation purposes let's take a look at how it is executed.

```
[aka@localhost ~]$ echo $PATH
/usr/local/sbin:/bin:/sbin:/usr/bin:/usr/sbin:/usr/loca
l/bin
```

You can add new directories to this string. Let's try it.

```
[aka@localhost ~]$ echo $PATH
/usr/local/sbin:/bin:/sbin:/usr/bin:/usr/sbin:/usr/loca
l/bin
[aka@localhost ~]$ PATH=$PATH:/home/rich/azuresky
[root@localhost ~]# echo $PATH
/usr/local/sbin:/bin:/sbin:/usr/bin:/usr/sbin:/usr/loca
l/bin:/home/rich/azuresky
[root@localhost ~]$
```

It is important to mention that each user in the Linux operating system has a different PATH variable than others. Upon installation of an operating system, a default variable for your PATH is set. After that, you can add more to it or completely change as it suits you.

Note: It is important to mention that the root user's PATH variable has more directories than any other user. An interesting thing about the PATH variable is that either you can change it just for the current session or on a permanent basis.

How to find Environment Variables of the Linux System

There are multiple variables that a system uses for identification purpose in the shell scripts. With the help of system variables, you can easily procure important information for the programs. There are different startup methods in the Linux system, and in each system, the bash shell executes the startup files in a different way.

The Login Shell

This locates four distinct startup files from where it could process its commands. The very first file that is executed is the */etc/profile*. You can dub it as the default file for the bash shell. Each you time you log in, this command will be executed.

```
[aka@localhost ~]# cat /etc/profile
# /etc/profile
```

I have run this command while logged in as a superuser. The result on your window can be slightly different.

Just take a look at the export command stated as under:

```
export PATH USER LOGNAME MAIL HOSTNAME HISTSIZE HISTCONTROL
```

You can clearly see that the export command ensures that the variables remain accessible to the child processes.

The $HOME

This one is a user-specific variable. Let's run it to know what it has got.

```
[aka@localhost ~]# cat .bash_profile
# .bash_profile

# Get the aliases and functions
if [ -f ~/.bashrc ]; then
        . ~/.bashrc
fi
```

```
# User specific environment and startup programs

PATH=$PATH:$HOME/bin

export PATH
```

Interactive Shell

If you happen to start the bash shell without first logging into the system, you kickstart the interactive shell. You have the command line to enter command here. With the start from an interactive shell, the system does not load the /etc/profile file. It locates another file called .bashrc in the home directory of the user. Let's see how this startup file looks in the Linux operating system.

```
[aka@localhost ~]# cat .bashrc
```

It conducts a couple of key tasks; first is checking for the bashrc file in the /etc directory. The second one is to allow the user to enter aliases.

```
[aka@localhost ~]$ cat /etc/bashrc
```

Variable Arrays

You can use variables as arrays. The fun thing with arrays is their capacity to hold multiple values which you can reference for a complete array. You can simply cram multiple values in a single variable by listing them with single spacing in parenthesis. Let's try it.

```
[aka@localhost ~]$ myworld=(one two three four five)
[aka@localhost ~]$ echo $myworld
one
[aka@localhost ~]$ echo ${myworld[2]}
three
[aka@localhost ~]$ echo ${myworld[1]}
two
```

```
[aka@localhost ~]$ echo ${myworld[4]}
five
```

You can see how easy it is to build up a variable array. You can bring out each value in the array with a special command. Now try the following to bring out the entire array.

```
[aka@localhost ~]$ echo ${myworld[*]}
one two three four five
```

In addition to this you can also unset a specific value from the array.

```
[aka@localhost ~]$ unset myworld[3]
[aka@localhost ~]$ echo ${myworld[*]}
one two three five
```

If you want to get rid of the entire array, you can do that by unsetting it.

```
[aka@localhost ~]$ unset myworld[*]
[aka@localhost ~]$ echo ${myworld[*]}

[aka@localhost ~]$
```

Variable arrays are not portable to other shell environments, that's why they are not the foremost option to be used with Linux operating system users.

CHAPTER 6

The Basics of Shell Scripting

Sylvia was too much excited to learn the basics of the Linux operating system and the command line. In fact, she found it quite amazing and satisfying to get the job done by entering a short command, getting immediate results, and just then I told her that the major part of the Linux system has yet to come. This is the toughest part for newbies. "So, will I have to code?" she asked when I alluded to the hard part of Linux. I replied in the affirmative. I will walk you through the world of shell scripting in this chapter. Shell scripting is much like coding. It is exciting, thrilling and creative.

You have learned by now to use the command line interface (CLI). You have entered commands and viewed the command results. Now the time is ripe for an advanced level of activity on Linux that is shell scripting in which you have to put in multiple commands and get results from each command. You can also transfer the result of one command to another. In short, you can pair up multiple commands in a single step. Let's how it is done.

Draft syntax like the following.

```
[aka@localhost ~]$ date ; who
```

Now run this command. You will have the date and time first and the details of the user who is currently logged in the system right under this command. You can add commands up to 255 characters. That's the final limit.

A tip: A problem will definitely get in your way when you try to combine multiple commands: remember them each time you have to enter them. An easy way to get rid of this issue is to save multiple commands into a text file so that you can copy and paste them when you need them. This definitely works for sure. You can also run the text file.

How to create a text file: You can create your customized file in the shell window and place shell command in the file. Open a text editor like vim to create a file. We have already practiced how to create a text file in Linux command line. Let's revise it.

```
[aka@localhost ~]$ cat > file.txt
The Statue Of Liberty Was Gifted By France.
```

So, get ready to draft your first shell script. Let's roll on. Open a bash text editor and draft the script as under or something similar like that.

```
#!bin/bash
# Script writing is interesting.
echo 'The sky is azure!'
```

The second with # in the start looks like a comment. In the third line, we can see the echo command. Remember that you have to ignore everything after the # sign.

Let's try it on in the command line.

```
[aka@localhost ~]$ echo 'The sky is azure!' #I have
entered a comment
The sky is azure!
```

Well, by now you might be thinking about the comments and their relation with the # sign. Then your mind will be distracted and perplexed to think about the first line of the script that also starts with the # sign. No, that's not a comment but rather a special line commonly known as *shebang*. This should come at the start of each script. You can save your file now with any name you desire. I saved it as *azure_sky*.

Displaying Messages

When you enter something in the command line, an output is definitely expected out of it that is displayed on the screen. You can also add text messages to let the user know what is going on in the script. The echo command does the wonder for you. It can show the string of simple text on the screen.

```
[aka@localhost ~]$ echo I hope you are writing the code
in the right way.
I hope you are writing the code in the right way.
[aka@localhost ~]$
```

Now let's try something exciting to see how it can go wrong and how to rectify what goes wrong.

```
[aka@localhost ~]$ echo I'll be happy if you don't go f
or swimming.
Ill be happy if you dont go for swimming.
[aka@localhost ~]$ echo "I'll be happy if you don't go
for swimming."
I'll be happy if you don't go for swimming.
[aka@localhost ~]$ echo 'John says "I'll be happy if yo
u don't go for swimming.
"'
John says "Ill be happy if you dont go for swimming."
[aka@localhost ~]$
```

The command went wrong, and the display was not what we had expected. So. We had to rectify it with the help of quotation marks.

Shall I Execute it Now?

It is time to execute the file you have just saved. Let's run the command.

```
[aka@localhost ~]$ azure_sky
bash: azure_sky: command not found
$
```

You have to guide the bash shell in locating your shell script file.

```
[aka@localhost ~]$ ls -1 azure_sky
-rw-r—r—1 me      me    63 2019-08-26 03:17 azure_sky
[aka@localhost ~]$ chmod 755 azure_sky
[aka@localhost ~]$ ls -1 azure_sky
rwxr-xr-x 1 me me 63 2019-08-26 03:17 azure_sky
```

But how will the command line find the script that you have just written? The script should have an explicit path name. In case you fail to do that, you are likely to see the following:

```
[aka@localhost ~]$ azure_sky
bash: azurer_sky: command not found
```

You must tell the command line the exact location of your script. Otherwise, you won't be able to execute it. There are different directories in the Linux system, and all of them are in the PATH variable. I have already shown you how to see what directories are on the system, explore the PATH variable.

```
[aka@localhost ~]$ echo $PATH
/usr/local/sbin:/bin:/sbin:/usr/bin:/usr/sbin:/usr/loca
l/bin:/home/rich/azuresky
[aka@localhost ~]$
```

Now that we have got the list of the directories you can see and put your script in the directory you want to. Follow the following steps to save your script in a specific directory.

```
[aka@localhost ~]$ mkdir bin
[aka@localhost ~]$ mv azure_sky bin
[aka@localhost ~]$ azure_sky
azure_sky
```

If your PATH variable misses the directory, you can add it by the following method:

```
[aka@localhost ~]$ export PATH=~/bin:"$PATH"
```

More ways to format scripts: The ultimate goal of a good script writer should be to write a good script and maintain it smoothly. You should be able to easily edit the script like adding more to a particular script or removing from it. Also, it should be formatted in a way that it should be easy to read as well as understand.

Go for long option names

We have seen many commands both with long and short options name. ls command that is used to list directories in your Linux system has lots of options such as the following:

```
[aka@localhost ~]$ ls -ad
[aka@localhost ~]$ ls -all --directory
```

Both these commands are equivalent when it comes to the results. Users prefer short options for ease of use so that they may not have to remember long option names. Almost every option that I have stated in previous chapters has a long form. Though short form options are easy to remember, it is always recommended to go for the full names when it comes to script writing because it is more reader-friendly.

Indentation

Now long form commands are also not very easy to handle. You have to take care to write them in the right format so that it may confuse the reader. You can use commas between many lines.

How to use Quotation Marks and Literals

This is quite technical. As a Linux user, you must know how and where to use quotation marks, commas and period. Why does a specific punctuation mark necessary for the script? Let us print the following string.

```
[aka@localhost ~]$ echo $100
00
```

The output should have been 100, but it was instead a double zero. If you are thinking that the command line couldn't understand the script and executed it what part it succeeded in comprehending, you are right. It got it all wrong. So, what should be done now? First, we need to understand why did it get it all wrong? Its reason is that the shell only saw 00. It considered $1 as a shell variable. That's what it is. You failed to make it easily readable. Perhaps you should add the quotation marks. Add them right away.

```
[aka@localhost ~]$ echo "$100"
00
```

You are getting it wrong. Still you get the same result. Are you frustrated by now? We have a solution.

```
[aka@localhost ~]$ echo '$100'
$100
```

We have got the result that we desired.

When you add the quotation marks to a script, you are on your way to creating a literal, which is a kind of string that runs through the command line fully intact. When you are looking forward to writing a script, you need to keep in mind that the shell analyzes the variables in a command before it runs it. It also performs substitutions if they must appear along the way, and when it is done with that, it forwards the results to the command line.

Let's see what problems may come your way when you are dealing with the literals. They can be more complicated than you might have thought. Let's assume you are looking into the /etc/passwd directory in order to locate the entries that match r.*t. This will help you locate usernames like the root and robot. See the command you will be using to execute your search.

```
[aka@localhost ~]# grep r.*t /etc/passwd
root:x:0:0:root:/root:/bin/bash
operator:x:11:0:operator:/root:/sbin/nologin
ftp:x:14:50:FTP User:/var/ftp:/sbin/nologin
systemd-
coredump:x:999:996:systemd Core Dumper:/:/sbin/nologin
systemd-
network:x:192:192:systemd Network Management:/:/sbin/no
login
systemd-
resolve:x:193:193:systemd Resolver:/:/sbin/nologin
tss:x:59:59:Account used by the trousers package to san
dbox the tcsd daemon:/dev
/null:/sbin/nologin
polkitd:x:998:995:User for polkitd:/:/sbin/nologin
sshd:x:74:74:Privilege-
separated SSH:/var/empty/sshd:/sbin/nologin
pesign:x:994:991:Group for the pesign signing daemon:/v
ar/run/pesign:/sbin/nolog
in
```

Well, it worked perfectly. When you execute the command, you will see that specific files are colored orange. It means you have got the information you were looking for. When it seems to be working fine, it fails sometimes for reasons unknown. That's why this trigger panic. If you are on the verge of getting panicked as Sylvia did when she did it all wrong, stop right there. The problem lies in your directories. Review them, and you will find the solution. In fact, let me walk you through the solution. If your directory has names like r.output and r.input, the command will not be able to interpret the command and the result will be like the one given as under:

```
[aka@localhost ~]$ grep r.output r.input /etc/passwd
```

If you want to keep a good distance from this kind of simple problems, you need to identify the characters that are likely to land you in trouble and also master the art of using quotation marks. A single mistake can put you away from the results you need.

Learning the use of single quotation marks:

As a Linux user, it might be frustrating to know that the shell is not going to leave the string alone. You might get fed up the constant interruptions of the shell toward the string. Single quotes, fortunately, can help you kill this frustration. Applying single quotes on your strings can solve the matter. Let's jump to the example.

```
[aka@localhost ~]$ grep 'r.*t' /etc/passwd
```

Why these single quotes matter much in solving the problem? The shell takes all the characters, including spaces inside the single quotes as a single parameter. This why if you enter the command without single quotes, it will not work. That's why when you are about to use a literal, you must turn to single quotes. Only in this way the shell will not attempt for substitutions.

As a matter of fact, the single quote marks operate as protectors for whatever you put inside them. You can say that it just kills the special meaning of the characters. In addition, the shell will be unable to accommodate variables and wildcards.

Mastering the art of the double quote marks.

Iin general, the double quotes just work like the single quotes. The only difference between the single and double quotes is that the latter is more flexible than the previous. For example, if you want to expand any variable inside the string, you should put the string inside the double quotation marks. Let's do it.

```
[aka@localhost ~]$ echo "There is no * on my path: $PAT
H"
There is no * on my path: /usr/local/sbin:/bin:/sbin:/u
sr/bin:/usr/sbin:/usr/loc
al/bin:/home/rich/azuresky
[aka@localhost ~]$
```

You can see that the double quotation marks have allowed the $PATH to expand but kept the (*) from the same act. So, whatever has a $ sign before it will be expanded when you run the command.

Food for thought: If you want only variable and command substitution to run, you should go for the double quotation marks. Please keep in mind that wildcards will still remain blocked.

The Backlash

The third option is the backlash. You can use it to alter the meaning that the characters carry. In addition, you can also use the option to escape any kind of special characters that are within the text, including the quote marks.

Most users find it tricky when they are about to pass the single quote to the command. To avoid any unexpected result, you should insert the backlash before the single quote marks.

```
[aka@localhost ~]$ "Path is \$PATH"
bash: Path is $PATH: command not found
[aka@localhost ~]$ "Path is $PATH"
bash: Path is /usr/local/sbin:/bin:/sbin:/usr/bin:/usr/
sbin:/usr/local/bin:/home
/rich/azuresky: No such file or directory
[aka@localhost ~]$
```

The important thing to keep in mind is that the backslash, as well as the quote, should remain outside the single quotes.

```
[aka@localhost ~]$ echo I don\'t like Italian food
I don't like Italian food
```

```
[aka@localhost ~]$ echo "I don't like Italian food"
I don't like Italian food
[aka@localhost ~]$ echo I don'\''t like Italian food'
I don\t like Italian food
[aka@localhost ~]$
```

Now you know how to get away from a syntax error with the help of backlash.

Decision Making in Linux: The Conditionals

For conditionals, the Bourne shell has special structures like *if/then/else* and *case* statements. The conditionals are all about decision making process in Linux. You can set Linux to make some decisions using bash shell. You have to set the conditions in order to make the system take certain decisions. Generally, a condition is an expression after the evaluates a certain statement as true or false.

Let's take a look at the *if* statement. If the system finds that the conditions that were set by the programmer are well met, it will allow the program to execute. Otherwise, it won't allow it. Let's take a look at the syntax of the *if* statement.

```
#!/bin/sh
if [$1 = the sky is definitely azure]; then
      echo 'The first argument was "the sky is
definitely azure"'
else
      echo -n 'The first argument was "the sky is
definitely azure"— '
      echo It was '"'$1'"'
fi
```

The above statement is for the single decision. For single decision, the statement can be as the following:

```
#!/bin/sh
if [$1 = the sky is definitely azure]; then
      echo 'The first argument was "the sky is
```

```
definitely azure"'
fi
```

For multiple decisions you can use the following statement.

```
#!/bin/sh
if [$1 = the sky is definitely azure]; then
        echo 'The first argument was "the sky is
definitely azure"'
```

then

```
[the condition 2]
else
        echo -n 'The first argument was "the sky is
definitely azure"- '
        echo It was '"'$1'"'
fi
```

How it goes can be understood by the following steps:

- First comes the *if* command. The shell runs it and collects the code you enter in the command.

- Remember the 1 and the 0. If the exit code is 0, the command stands executed and you will see the then keyword, ending up at the *else* or *fi* keyword. The whole process ends in *fi*.

Let's take a look at the expanded version of the *if* command. I'll add *elif* (else-if) in the expanded version.

```
NAME="AHSAN"
if ["$NAME" = "SYLVIA"]; then
    echo "SYLVIA ADAMS"
elif ["$NAME" = "AHSAN"]; then
    echo "AHSAN SHAH"
else
    echo "It boils down to Adam and Jack"
fi
```

The problem with the conditional

Now we should talk about a slight glitch in the conditional statement. When you enter the above conditional statement, it may not run as you think just because $1 could be empty. You might have missed setting a parameter which results in aborting the command with an error altogether, but you can fix the problem by taking the following measures.

```
if ["$1" = the sky is azure]
then

if [ x"$1" = x"hi"]
then
```

The *if* command is versatile when it comes to using different commands.

Testing the conditionals with other commands

When you enter *if* in the shell window, whatever comes next to it is considered as a command. This helps us understand why we put a semicolon before *then*. If we don't do that, we will have to write on the next line. Let's add some other commands into the conditionals.

```
[aka@localhost ~]# if grep -q daemon /etc/passwd; then
> echo The user is hidden in the password file.
> else
> echo Look somewhere else. It is not in the password f
ile.
> fi
```

&& and ||

The first one as expected means *and* while the second construct means *or*. Let's see how you can run these commands.

firstcommand && secondcomman

Suppose the shell runs *command1* and the exit code turns out to be zero, the shell moves on to the second command in the construct and runs it.

The || construct is different from && in a way that it runs the second command even if the first command returns an exit code with a nonzero value.

```
[aka@localhost ~]# if [ahsan] && [sylvia]; then
> echo "both can go to the concert"
> elif [ahsan] || [sylvia]
> echo "only one can go to the concert"
> fi
```

More if-then features

The *if* command has gone an extra mile to fulfill users' expectations. You can add much more to the logical decision making. Some of the advanced features include the following:

- Double parenthesis

- Double square brackets

How and where to use double parenthesis

Double parenthesis command is amazing in a sense that it allows Linux users to use mathematical formulas in the script. You can add some advanced mathematical symbols in the script just like other programmers do while coding. This allows users more freedom while composing scripts. Let's move on right away to the syntax to make things clear.

```
[aka@localhost ~]$ #!/bin/bash
[aka@localhost ~]$ #using double parenthesis
[aka@localhost ~]$ val1=5
[aka@localhost ~]$ if ((val1 ** 4 > 50)); then
```

```
> ((val2=$val1**2))
> echo "The square of $val1 is $val2"
> fi
The square of 5 is 25
[aka@localhost ~]$
```

Other command symbols you can use in the above script are given as under:

- Pre-increment : ++val

- Logical negation: !

- Right bitwise shift: >>

- Left bitwise shift: <<

- Post-increment: val++

- Bitwise negation: ~

- Logical AND: &&

- Logical OR: ||

The double brackets

Now the next special feature is the use of double brackets. This command is used in string comparisons. Its special use is in pattern matching.

```
[aka@localhost ~]$ #!/bin/bash
[aka@localhost ~]$ #using pattern bashing
[aka@localhost ~]$ if [[$USER == r*]]
> then
> echo "Hey $USER"
> else "I cannot recognize you. Come back later."
> fi
```

If the command inside the double bracket matches the $USER variable and finds that it starts with the letter *r*, which in this case is *rae*, then the shell obviously executes the *then* section part of the script.

The Loops

Sylvia happens to be a Marvel fan. She never misses a single movie. One of her favorite characters is Doctor Strange, the accidental wizard. Well, I don't like these fantasy things but why I am talking about it is the fact that one day Sylvia half narrated and half described by gestures a scene from one his movies in which he fabricates by his magic a time loop to defeat the villain Dormamu. I loved the tale because of its sprightliness. Sylvia loved it more because she connected it with the loops in Linux. Doctor Strange traps Dormamu in a time loop in which he was supposed to remain endlessly until he agreed to Dr. Strange's bargain. Again, and again Dr. Strange appears and is killed by Dormamu because of the time loop which keeps repeating itself.

Sylvia linked the two loops and fed the lesson in her mind quite successfully. A smart thought though she could have understood it without Marvel. Let's see how it goes. Jump right away to the script.

```
[aka@localhost ~]$ #!/bin/sh
[aka@localhost ~]$ for str in earth sun mars moon satur
n;do
> echo $str
> done
earth
sun
mars
moon
saturn
[aka@localhost ~]$
```

In the above, you can notice that the above script is a combination of different words. While some may seem familiar to you, others are difficult to interpret. Out of the above *for, done, in,* and *do* are shell keywords. Let me explain in words how the loop works.

There is a variable *str* in the above script. When you enter the above text in the shell window, the shell fills the variable with the value of the first of the space-delimited values that can be seen above after the shell keyword *in.* The first word here is *earth.* Then the shell executes the echo command. After that, the shell once again returns back to the *for* line to set fill in the variable with the next value that is in this case *sun.* It repeats the same exercise with the second value. The loop goes on until there is no value left written after the keyword *in.*

The *for* command fills in the variable with whatever the next values are in the list. We can use the *str* variable like any other variable in shell scripting. When the last of the iterations are done, the *str* variable keeps the last value it was filled with. Here an interesting thing is that you can change that. Let's see how to do that.

```
$ cat testfile
#!/bin/bash
# testing the for variable after the looping
for str in earth sun mars saturn
do
echo "The next planet is $str"
done
echo "The next planet to visit is $str"
str=Uranus
echo "We are going to $str"
$ ./testfile
The next state is earth
The next state is sun
The next state is mars
The next state is saturn
The next planet to visit is Uranus
We are going to Uranus
$
```

The *for* loop is always not that easy to use. Simple problems in the syntax can push you over the edge and you will land in utter darkness with no clue on what to do. Do you want to see an example? Let's do that.

```
$ cat testfile
#!/bin/bash
# example of the wrong use of the for command
for test in I was pretty sure it'll work but I don't
know what went wrong
do
echo "word:$str"
done
$ ./testfile
word:I was pretty sure
word:itll work but I dont
word:know what went wrong
$
```

The single quote marks did the damage in the above script. This kind of error really catches the programmer off-guard. To resolve the problem, you can use backslash or double quotation marks to properly define the values. Another problem is the use of multiword.

```
[aka@localhost ~]$ #!/bin/bash
[aka@localhost ~]$ #another wrong use of the for comman
d
[aka@localhost ~]$ for str in The Netherlands Australia
 The United States Of America Scotland The British
> do
> echo "I will visit $str"
> done
I will visit The
I will visit Netherlands
I will visit Australia
I will visit The
I will visit United
I will visit States
I will visit Of
I will visit America
```

105

```
I will visit Scotland
I will visit The
I will visit British
[aka@localhost ~]$
```

Now let's see how to do it right by making use of the double quotation marks in the script. You will be astonished to see how simple it is to rectify it.

```
[aka@localhost ~]$ #!/bin/bash
[aka@localhost ~]$ #How to do it right
[aka@localhost ~]$ for str in "The Netherlands" Austral
ia "The United States Of
 America" Scotland "The British"; do echo "I will visit
 $str"; done
I will visit The Netherlands
I will visit Australia
I will visit The United States Of America
I will visit Scotland
I will visit The British
[aka@localhost ~]$
```

How about reading a list with the help of a variable?

Suppose you have a list of values that are stored in a variable. You can use the *for* command to iterate through the list.

```
[akalocalhost ~]$ #!/bin/bash
[aka@localhost ~]$ #we will use the for command to deal
 with the list
[aka@localhost ~]$ list="Hands Face Hair Feet Limbs Elb
ows"
[aka@localhost ~]$ list=$list"neck"
[aka@localhost ~]$ for parts in $list
> do
> echo "I have washed my $list"
> done
I have washed my Hands
I have washed my Face
I have washed my Hair
I have washed my Feet
```

```
I have washed my Limbs
I have washed my Elbows
I have washed my neck
[aka@localhost ~]$
```

The While Loop

There is another loop named as the *while* loop. Let's look at the syntax of the bash while loop.

```
[aka@localhost ~]# while [fill the condition in the
brackets]
do
        sample commandx
        sample commandy
        sample commandz
done
```

All the commands in between *do* and *done* are executed repeatedly until the condition stands true.

```
[aka@localhost ~]$ #!/bin/bash
[aka@localhost ~]$ x=1
[aka@localhost ~]$ while [$x -le 10]
> do
> echo "the sky is azure $x times"
> x=$(($x+1))
> done
```

The Case Statement

The *case* statement is dissimilar to a loop. There is no such thing as repetition in the *case* command. You can test simple values such as integers as well as characters. In a *case* command, the bash shell analyzes the condition and accordingly manages the program flow. The case statement at first expands whatever expression you include in it and then it tries to match the same against the patterns that are included in the script. If it founds a match, all the statements ending up at the double semicolon (;;) get executed by the shell. When it is

107

done, the case stands terminated with the exit status that you had given to the last command. If the *case* command finds no match, the exit status stands at zero.

```
$ cat testfile
#!/bin/bash
# using the case command
case $USER in
sylvia | john)
echo "Welcome, $USER"
echo "Have a nice time";;
testing)
echo "Special testing account";;
adam)
echo "Keep in mind to log off when you have finished
the task";;
*)
echo "You cannot enter";;
esac
$ ./testfile
Welcome, sylvia
Have a nice time
$
```

In the above script, we can clearly see that a variable is compared against different sets of patterns. If there is a match between the variable and the pattern, the related command is executed. The catch here is that the *case* command offers us a smoother way of integrating different options for a specific variable. Let's write the same script using the *if-then* statement.

```
$ cat testfile
#!/bin/bash
# looking for a possible value
if [ $USER = "sylvia" ]
then
echo "Welcome $USER"
echo "Have a nice time"
elif [ $USER = john ]
then
```

```
echo "Welcome $USER"
echo "Have a nice time"
elif [ $USER = testing ]
then
echo "Special testing account"
elif [ $USER = adam ]
then
echo " Keep in mind to log off when you have finished
the task "
else
echo "You cannot enter"
fi
$ ./testfile
Welcome sylvia
Please enjoy your visit
$
```

I hope you have understood by now the difference between both scripts. The *case* command just puts all the values in a single list form which the variable checks it for a match. You don't have to write *elif* statements. The repetition is eliminated.

So, what have we learned so far with different scripts? The above commands are also known as structured commands. We can alter the normal program flow in the shell script with the help of these commands. The most basic of these commands is the *if-then* statement. You can evaluate a command and move on to execute other commands on the basis of the result of the evaluated command.

You have the option of connecting different *if-then* statements with the help of *elif* statement. The *elif* is the short of *else if* which means it is another *if-then* statement. The *case* command can be dubbed as the shortest route to achieving the same results as we have with the help of using lengthy *if-then* statements.

Nesting loops

Now this is simple. You can combine different loops into one or you can nest other loops in an already established one. The good thing is that you can add as many loops as you can for nesting.

```
[aka@localhost ~]$ #!/bin/bash
[aka@localhost ~]$ #Testing nested loops
[aka@localhost ~]$ for ((b=1; b<=6; b++))
> do
> echo "Starting loop $b:"
> for ((d=1; d<=6; d++))
> do
> echo "Inside loop: $d"
> done
> done
Starting loop 1:
Inside loop: 1
Inside loop: 2
Inside loop: 3
Inside loop: 4
Inside loop: 5
Inside loop: 6
Starting loop 2:
Inside loop: 1
Inside loop: 2
Inside loop: 3
Inside loop: 4
Inside loop: 5
Inside loop: 6
Starting loop 3:
Inside loop: 1
Inside loop: 2
Inside loop: 3
Inside loop: 4
Inside loop: 5
Inside loop: 6
Starting loop 4:
Inside loop: 1
Inside loop: 2
Inside loop: 3
```

```
Inside loop: 4
Inside loop: 5
Inside loop: 6
Starting loop 5:
Inside loop: 1
Inside loop: 2
Inside loop: 3
Inside loop: 4
Inside loop: 5
Inside loop: 6
Starting loop 6:
Inside loop: 1
Inside loop: 2
Inside loop: 3
Inside loop: 4
Inside loop: 5
Inside loop: 6
[aka@localhost ~]$
```

So you can see the nested loop inside the main loop tends to iterate through its values each time as the outer loop or main loop iterates. Don't get confused between the *dos* and *dones* of the script. Bash shell differentiates the two and refers them to the inner and outer loops. In the above script I blended together two *for* loops. Now let's move on to pair up a *for* and a *while* loop.

```
#!/bin/bash
# filling in a for loop inside a while loop
a=5
while [ $a -ge 0 ]
do
echo "Outer loop: $a"
for (( b = 1; $b < 3; b++ ))
do
c=$[ $a * $b ]
echo " Inner loop: $a * $b = $c"
done
a=$[ $a - 1 ]
done
$ ./test15
```

111

```
Outer loop: 5
Inner loop: 5 * 1 = 5
Inner loop: 5 * 2 = 10
Outer loop: 4
Inner loop: 4 * 1 = 4
Inner loop: 4 * 2 = 8
Outer loop: 3
Inner loop: 3 * 1 = 3
Inner loop: 3 * 2 = 6
Outer loop: 2
Inner loop: 2 * 1 = 2
Inner loop: 2 * 2 = 4
Outer loop: 1
Inner loop: 1 * 1 = 1
Inner loop: 1 * 2 = 2
Outer loop: 0
Inner loop: 0 * 1 = 0
Inner loop: 0 * 2 = 0
$
```

The break Command

The break command, as is evident from the name, is used to break out of the loop by terminating the same. It is applicable on the *for, while* and *until* loop. It can also be dubbed as the escape command.

```
#!/bin/bash
# Time to break out of a loop
for a in 1 2 3 4 5 6 7 8 9 10
do
if [ $a -eq 8 ]
then
break
fi
echo "Iteration number: $a"
done
echo "The for loop is completed"
Iteration number: 1
Iteration number: 2
Iteration number: 3
Iteration number: 4
```

```
Iteration number: 5
Iteration number: 6
Iteration number: 7
The for loop is completed
$
```

The loop was broken from the very point I asked it to. Now I'll break out of the inner loop I have written.

```
$ cat testfile
#!/bin/bash
# I am breaking out of an inner loop
for (( x = 1; a < 4; a++ ))
do
echo "Outer loop: $x"
for (( y = 1; y < 100; y++ ))
do
if [ $y -eq 5 ]
then
break
fi
echo " Inner loop: $y"
done
done
$ ./testfile
Outer loop: 1
Inner loop: 1
Inner loop: 2
Inner loop: 3
Inner loop: 4
Outer loop: 2
Inner loop: 1
Inner loop: 2
Inner loop: 3
Inner loop: 4
Outer loop: 3
Inner loop: 1
Inner loop: 2
Inner loop: 3
Inner loop: 4
$
```

Let's see how to break out of an outer loop.

```
$ cat testfile
#!/bin/bash
# How to break out of an outer loop
for (( e = 1; e < 4; e++ ))
do
echo "Outer loop: $a"
for (( f = 1; f < 100; f++ ))
do
if [ $f -gt 4 ]
then
break 2
fi
echo " Inner loop: $f"
done
done
$ ./testfile
Outer loop: 1
Inner loop: 1
Inner loop: 2
Inner loop: 3
Inner loop: 4
$
```

The Continue Command

This command is somewhat related to the break command, as it also terminates the processing of the loop, but differs from the break command because it doesn't exit the loop. You can set your own conditions in the script to direct the loop to stop where you want it to be.

```
$ cat testfile
#!/bin/bash
# testing the continue command
for (( x = 1; x < 15; x++ ))
do
if [ $x -gt 5 ] && [ $x -lt 10 ]
then
```

```
continue
fi
echo "The Numeric Digit: $x"
done
$ ./testfile
The Numeric Digit: 1
The Numeric Digit: 2
The Numeric Digit: 3
The Numeric Digit: 4
The Numeric Digit: 5
The Numeric Digit: 10
The Numeric Digit: 11
The Numeric Digit: 12
The Numeric Digit: 13
The Numeric Digit: 14
$
```

Processing the Output of a Loop

The shell gives you an opportunity to redirect the output of your loop to a particular file. You have to fill in the shell window with the script you have in mind. You have to create a file when the loop ends. Your output from the loop script is secured inside a text file that you create. It will look easier when you will practice it. Let's jump right into the shell window.

```
[aka@localhost ~]$ #!/bin/bash
[aka@localhost ~]$ #redirecting the output of the loop
toward a file
[aka@localhost ~]$ for ((x=1 ; x<10;x++))
> do
> echo "the numeric digit is $x"
> done > azuresky.txt
[aka@localhost ~]$ echo "the command is finished."
the command is finished.
[aka@localhost ~]$ cat azuresky.txt
the numeric digit is 1
the numeric digit is 2
the numeric digit is 3
the numeric digit is 4
```

115

```
the numeric digit is 5
the numeric digit is 6
the numeric digit is 7
the numeric digit is 8
the numeric digit is 9
[aka@localhost ~]$
```

A similar technique can be used to pipe the output of your loop script to the command you want to. Let's experiment with this.

```
[aka@localhost ~]$ #!/bin/bash
[aka@localhost ~]$ #Piping out the output
[aka@localhost ~]$ for country in "The Netherlands" Aus
tralia Pakistan Spain "The United States of America"
> do
> echo "This summer I'll visit $country"
> done | sort
This summer I'll visit Australia
This summer I'll visit Pakistan
This summer I'll visit Spain
This summer I'll visit The Netherlands
This summer I'll visit The United States of America
[aka@localhost ~]$
```

CHAPTER 7

Moving On To The Advanced Level In Shell Scripting

W When you get used to writing shell scripts, you will be able to use your own scripts somewhere else to execute a program. A small code can be integrated into another script to get the desired result. Writing large scripts can be an exhaustive exercise to do that's why the shell offers programmers a convenient way to do script writing. There are user-defined functions that can make script writing easy and fun.

The Shell Functions

Shell functions save you from repeat writing the same code for different tasks. Displaying messages and doing mathematical calculations can be tedious for you when you have to do that over and over again.

With shell functions, you can write once and then use the block of code over and over again.

How to Create Function

You can use two formats to create functions in bash shell scripts. The first format can be dissected into the keyword 'function' and the name that you assign to the block of the code. See the syntax as under:

```
function name that you will assign to the block code {
    commands
}
```

The name means the unique name you assign to your particular function. The commands can be a single or multiple bash command. You can add many or as little command as you desire. Just call the function and it will execute the commands in the order you in which you place them in the script. The function command doesn't add to or cut from the performance of the script. It just flows in the normal order.

How to Use the Function Script

When you are about to use the function command, don't forget to assign it a name. Let's see an example.

```
$ cat testfile
#!/bin/bash
# Let's see how to use a function in a script
function functest1 {
echo "Let's see how function works"
}
count=1
while [ $count -le 5 ]
do
functest1
count=$[ $count + 1 ]
done
echo "The loop ends here"
functest1
echo "this makes the end of this script"
$ ./testfile
Let's see how function works
Let's see how function works
Let's see how function works
Let's see how function works
```

```
Let's see how function works
The loop ends here
Let's see how function works
this makes the end of this script
$
```

You can see that each time you refer back to the functest1, the function that you have named, the bash shell gets back to the same to execute the commands you had left in there. That means you are saved from the hassle of repeating the script in the command line. Just remember the unique name that you assign to the function. I hope you have understood by now why the name is so important.

You don't have to write the shell function in the start. Instead, you can also write in in the middle of the script. But you have to define the function before using it, otherwise you will get an error message. Let's see an example.

```
$ cat testfile
#!/bin/bash
# put the shell function in the middle of the script
count=1
echo "This line is placed before the function
definition"
function functest1 {
echo "Now this is just a function"
}
while [ $count -le 5 ]
do
functest2
count=$[ $count + 1 ]
done
echo "The loop has reached its end"
func2
echo "This heralds the end of the script"
function func2 {
echo "Now this is just a function example"
}
$ ./testfile
This line comes before the function definition
```

```
Now this is just a function example
Now this is just a function example
Now this is just a function example
Now this is just a function example
Now this is just a function example
The loop has reached its end
./testfile: functest2: command not found
This heralds the end of the script
$
```

I defined the functest1 later in the script and when I used it, it ran okay, but I didn't define functest2 before using it, so it results in an error message. A thing which you should be careful about is the name of the functions. You should not assign the same name to different functions. Each function must have a unique name, otherwise, the shell will not be able to identify them separately, and will override the previous definition with the new one. Remember, there won't be any error messages to alert you about the mistake you are committing.

```
$ cat testfile
#!/bin/bash
# using the same name for different functions
function functest1 {
echo "I am defining the function with a unique name"
}
functest1
function functest1 {
echo "I have repeated the function name assigning it to
another function"
}
functest1
echo "The script ends here"
$ ./testfile
I am defining the function with a unique name
I have repeated the function name assigning it to
another function
The script ends here
$
```

How to return a value using shell functions

If we talk about the default exit status, it is the exit status which is returned by the last command of the function.

```
$ cat testfile
#!/bin/bash
# learning about the exit status of a shell function
functest1() {
echo "I am attempting to display a file which is non-
existent"
ls -l badfile
}
echo "it is time to test the function:"
functest1
echo "The exit status is: $?"
$ ./testfile
it is time to test the function:
I am attempting to display a file which is non-existent
ls: badfile: No such file or directory
The exit status is: 1
$
```

The exit status turns out to be 1 since the last command has failed.

```
$ cat testfile
#!/bin/bash
# time to test the exit status of a shell function
func1() {
ls -l badfile
echo "We should now test a bad command"
}
echo "shall we test the function now:"
func1
echo "The exit status is: $?"
$ ./test4b
shall we test the function now:
ls: badfile: No such file or directory
We should now test a bad command
The exit status is: 0
$
```

How to use the function output

We have seen how to capture and process the output of a shell variable. Now I'll explain how you can capture a function's output.

```
$ cat testfile
#!/bin/bash
# I will use the echo command to return a value
function dbl {
read -p "Enter a value: " value
echo $[ $value * 5 ]
}
result=`dbl`
echo "The new value is $result"
$ ./testfile
Enter a value: 300
The new value is 1500
$ ./testfile
Enter a value: 500
The new value is 2500
$
```

The echo will display the result of the mathematical calculation. The script gets the value of dbl function instead of locating the exit status as the final answer. So, we have redirected the shell to capture the output of the function.

How to Pass Parameters to a Shell Function

Functions can use the standard parameter environment variables for the representation of any parameters which are passed on to the function on the CLI. $0 variable is used to represent the definition of the function. Other parameters are $1, $2,$3 and so on are used to define the parameters on the command line. There also is a special variable $# in order to determine the total number of parameters on the command line. The parameters should be written on the same command line on which you are writing the function.

```
$ cat testfile
```

```
#!/bin/bash
# how to pass parameters to a function
function addem {
if [ $# -eq 0 ] || [ $# -gt 2 ]
then
echo -1
elif [ $# -eq 1 ]
then
echo $[ $1 + $1 ]
else
echo $[ $1 + $2 ]
fi
}
echo -n "Adding 20 and 30: "
value=`addem 20 30`
echo $value
echo -n "Shall we try to add only one number: "
value=`addem 20`
echo $value
echo -n "This time try to add no numbers: "
value=`addem`
echo $value
echo -n "Let's add three numbers this time: "
value=`addem 20 30 40`
echo $value
$ ./test6
Adding 20 and 30: 50
Let's try adding just one number: 40
Now trying adding no numbers: -1
Finally, try adding three numbers: -1
$
```

The shell acted as it was told. Where there were more than two parameters, it returns the value of -1. Where there was one parameter, it added the figure to itself. Where there were two parameters, it added them together to get the result.

How to use global variables in a shell function

The variables have a versatile use which makes them often confusing to learn. You can also use them in the shell functions. They have a different role here. You can use the following variables in the shell functions.

- **Global**

- **Local**

Global variables are valid within the shell script. Even if you define its value in the main script, you can retrieve its value in the function.

```
$ cat testfile
#!/bin/bash
# how to use a global variable to pass a value
function dbl {
vle=$[ $vle * 2 ]
}
read -p "Enter a vle: " vle
dbl
echo "The new value is: $vle"
$ ./testfile
Enter a vle: 300
The new vle is: 600
$
```

Don't get confused I have used vle instead of value. The variable $vle is defined here in the main script but is still valid inside the function.

```
$ cat testfile
#!/bin/bash
# let's see how things can go real bad by the wrong use
of variables
function functest1 {
temp=$[ $value + 5 ]
result=$[ $temp * 2 ]
}
```

```
temp=4
value=6
functest1
echo "We have the result as $result"
if [ $temp -gt $value ]
then
echo "temp is larger"
else
echo "temp is smaller"
fi
$ ./badtest2
The result is 22
temp is larger
$
```

Local variables are also used in functions. Local variables are mostly used internally. Put the keyword *local* before the variable declaration. You can make use of the local variable while you are assigning a value to the variable. With the help of the keyword, it becomes easier for the shell to identify the local variable inside the function script. If any variable of the same name appears outside of the function script, the shell considers it of separate value.

```
[aka@localhost ~]$ #!/bin/bash
[aka@localhost ~]$ #I will attempt to an array variable
[aka@localhost ~]$ function functest1 { echo "The param
eters are: $@"; thisarray=$1; echo "the array is ${myar
ray[*]}";
}
[aka@localhost ~]# myarray=(1 2 3 4 5 6 7 8 9)
[aka@localhost ~]# ehco "the original array is ${myarra
y[*]}"
functest1 $myarray
$ ./testfile
The original array is: 1 2 3 4 5 6 7 8 9
The parameters are: 1
./testfile: thisarray[*]: bad array subscript
The received array is
$
```

You must allot the array variable its individual values and then use those values as function parameters.

```
[aka@localhost ~]$ #!/bin/bash
[aka@localhost ~]$ #I will attempt to an array variable
[aka@localhost ~]$ function functest1 {
local newarray
newarray=('echo "$@"')
echo "The value for the array is: ${newarray[*]}"
}
[aka@localhost ~]# myarray=(1 2 3 4 5 6 7 8 9)
[aka@localhost ~]# ehco "the original array is ${myarra
y[*]}"
functest1 ${myarray[*]}
$ ./testfile
The original array is: 1 2 3 4 5 6 7 8 9
The new array is: 1 2 3 4 5 6 7 8 9
$
```

How to create a library using functions

This can be really handy if you are an administrative assistant at an office. You will save plenty of time that would otherwise have been spent on typing repeated scripts. You can create a library file to use as many times as you deem fit.

```
$ cat libfile
# creating a library file using shell functions
function addem {
echo $[ $2 + $3 ]
}
function multem {
echo $[ $5 * $2 ]
}
function divem {
if [ $2 -ne 0 ]
then
echo $[ $1 / $2 ]
else
echo -1
```

```
fi
}
$
```

You can now fill in the library file name in the script and get the desired output.

```
$ cat testfile
#!/bin/bash
# how to use functions you have defined in the library
file
. ./libfile
val1=20
val2=10
result1=`addem $val1 $val2`
result2=`multem $val1 $val2`
result3=`divem $val1 $val2`
echo "The result of adding them is: $result1"
echo "The result of multiplying them is: $result2"
echo "The result of dividing them is: $result3"
$ ./testfile
The result of adding them is: 30
The result of multiplying them is: 200
The result of dividing them is: 2
$
```

Use the Functions on the Command Line

Let's learn using the functions on the command line.

```
$ function divem { echo $[ $1 / $2 ]; }
$ divem 200 10
20
$

$ function doubleit { read -p "Enter val: " val; echo
$[
$ val * 5 ]; }
$ doubleit
Enter value: 50
225
```

```
$

$ function multem {
> echo $[ $1 * $2 ]
> }
$ multem 100 100
10000
$
```

Shell functions are a great way to place script code in a single place so that you can it repeatedly whenever needed. It eliminates the rewriting practice. If you have to use a lot of functions in order to deal with some heavy workload, you have the option to create function libraries.

How to create text menus in the shell

It is time to make shell scripting more interesting by making scripting interactive. This is pure programming. You can offer your customers an interactive menu display to choose from if you are tired of dealing with them all day at the office. Linux can make this fun.

Obviously, you need to have the layout first for then menu. You can add what you want to be included in the menu. Before creating the menu, it is a good idea to run the clear command. After that, you can enter the echo command to display different elements of your menu.

You can add newline characters and the tab with the help of -e command. The command line by default displays only printable characters.

```
clear
echo
echo -e "\t\t\tWelcome to the Admin Menu\n"
echo -e "\t1. Her will be displayed the disk space"
echo -e "\t2. Here will be displayed the logged on
users"
```

```
echo -e "\t3. Here will be displayed the memory usage"
echo -e "\t0. Exit\n\n"
echo -en "\t\tEnter your option: "
```

With the -en option in the last line, there will be no newline character in the end of the display. This will allow the users to enter their input. You can retrieve and read the input left by the customer with the help of the following command.

```
read -n 1 option
```

You can assign functions to the menu. These functions are pretty fun to do. The key is to create separate functions for each item in your menu. In order to save yourself the hassle, create stub functions so that you know what you have to put in there while you work smoothly in the shell. A full function will not be kept from running in the shell, which will interrupt your working. Working would be smoother if you put the entire menu in a function script.

```
function menu {
clear
echo
echo -e "\t\t\tWelcome to the Admin Menu\n"
echo -e "\t1. Her will be displayed the disk space"
echo -e "\t2. Here will be displayed the logged on
users"
echo -e "\t3. Here will be displayed the memory usage"
echo -e "\t0. Exit\n\n"
echo -en "\t\tEnter your option: "
read -n 1 option
}
```

As I have already discussed, this will help you to view the menu anytime by just recalling the function command. Now you need the case command to integrate the layout and the function to make the menu work in real time.

```
$ cat menu1
#!/bin/bash
```

```
# simple script menu
function diskspace {
clear
df -k
}
function whoseon {
clear
who
}
function memusage {
clear
cat /proc/meminfo
}
function themenu {
clear
echo
echo -e "\t\t\tWelcome to the Admin Menu\n"
echo -e "\t1. Her will be displayed the disk space"
echo -e "\t2. Here will be displayed the logged on
users"
echo -e "\t3. Here will be displayed the memory usage"
echo -e "\t0. Exit\n\n"
echo -en "\t\tEnter your option: "
read -n 1 option
}
while [ 1 ]
do
menu
case $option in
0)
break ;;
1)
diskspace ;;
2)
whoseon ;;
3)
memusage ;;
*)
clear
echo "Sorry, you went for the wrong selection";;
esac
```

```
echo -en "\n\n\t\t\tHit any key on the keyboard to
continue"
read -n 1 line
done
clear
$
```

Conclusion

Sylvia is an avid learner by now. She admits that what she had hated all her life has become her lifeline. The ease of use, the speed, the power over her computer, and the fun that Linux gave her was matchless. She has now installed Linux on her personal computer at home. Sylvia is now on her way to becoming a Linux pro. I wonder if she would soon be able to advise me on the command line because of the way she practices the shell. A trick she would never tell anyone is that she kept a diary on which she wrote all the important commands in order to easily invoke them when she needed them. Eventually, it helped her memorize the commands.

Linux is an operating system just like you have Windows or Mac OS X. Some say that it floats between the software and the hardware form of the operating system. Linux is considered better than the Windows operating system by programmers and white hat hackers. On the other hand, ordinary folks who have to deal with routine office work or play games prefer the Windows operating system. Linux is definitely better than Windows and there are reasons behind the notion. Let's analyze them so that you have a clearer mind with respect to different operating systems when you finish reading this book.

It is pertinent to cite an example. What if you buy a high-end phone but are unable to see what is inside it and how does it operate? Windows operating system is just like that phone. You can use it, enjoy it, but you cannot see how it works, how it is powered, and how it is wired. On the contrary, Linux is open-source. You can get into its source code any time you like.

The world is moving very fast when it comes to technology. While there are good people across the world who are adding positive things to the cyber world, such as operating systems and applications that can really help you deal with day to day activities, there is no shortage of the bad ones who are consistently trying to sneak into your personal computer to rob you of any important piece of information that could help them get some each money. It is now your foremost priority to protect yourself from the people who harbor such heinous designs. The basic thing to have that protection is to get the operating system that is secure against any such attacks.

Windows OS is extremely vulnerable to hacking attacks. I cannot claim that Linux is absolutely impenetrable but still it is much better than the Windows. Its features such as the package management and repositories make it securer than Windows. If you have Windows OS installed on your personal computer, you consistently run the risk of catching virus on your system that's why the first thing you do after installing the Windows OS is to purchase an antivirus program in order to keep your computer well-protected. However, with Linux on your personal computer, this need is eliminated.

Windows OS is very sensitive about the specifications of the system on which it is to be installed. For example, to get Windows 10 installed on your system, you need to update your RAM and HDD capacity. My friend had a laptop with Windows 7 installed on it. Suddenly, his system started showing the message that Microsoft Windows had stopped supporting Windows 7 and that's he must install Windows 10 on the computer. The message also read a caution that it was better to purchase a new computer on which Windows 10 was already installed by the company. That was under the heading of recommended action. As most people would have done, he bought a new computer and sold the old one.

This is absolutely not the case with Linux. All you need is to meet up the minimum system requirements and start the operating system without any fear of its expiration. Linux has the power to revive old computer systems. If you have a system with 256 MB RAM and an old processor, that is enough to run Linux. Now compare that with Windows 10 which demands 8GB RAM for smooth functioning. If you give the same system specifications to the Linux operating system, it would surely give you an edge over the Windows OS.

In addition, Linux is best for programmers. It supports all programming languages such as Java, Python, Ruby, Perl and C++. Additionally, there is a wide range of apps that suit programmers. Especially the package manager on Linux is what the programmer needs to get things done smoothly.

Linux offers a wide range of software updates, which are faster to install, unlike Windows which restarts multiple times just to install latest updates. Apart from the all benefits, the greatest of all is the option of customization. Whatever you get in the Windows is the ultimate truth. You cannot change it for your ease of use. With Linux things change dramatically. You can customize different features. You can add or delete different features of the operating system at will. Keep what you need and delete what you don't like because it is an open source system. Also, you can add or dispose of various wallpapers and icon theme on your system in order to customize its look.

Perhaps the greatest benefits with Linux is that you can get it for free online. Unlike the Windows OS you don't have to purchase it.

This book helps users in learning the basics of Linux command line interface, which makes Linux different from all the other operating systems. Now that you have made it till the end, I hope that you have learned what makes Linux fun to use. I hope that the dread of the command line interface, the dark screen I talked about in the introduction, has vanished into thin air.

It is not that boring. You can do more work with Linux in a short timeframe which makes it fun to use. Linux provides you flexibility with respect to components you need to install. You can what you require and leave what you don't. For example, you can do away with unnecessary programs like paint and boring calculators in Windows. Instead, you can take any important and relevant program from the open source, write it on the command line and run it on the system. You can add and delete programs and applications as many as you like.

If the Windows OS catches a malware, it corrupts leaving you at the mercy of luck. If the system survives the attack, you get your data back. If it doesn't, you can only mourn your loss and do nothing. You don't have any backup for the Windows OS in any other partition; a backup that could keep forming an image of what you are doing on the operating system to save it for the day you get the OS corrupted by an attack. But Linux offers you the perfect solution. You can keep Linux file in multiple partitions. If one of them corrupts, you can access your data from the other partitions. That's simple and handy.

I hope this book has provided you with the basic knowledge you need to move further on the ladder in the world of Linux. I cannot promise that a single read of this book will make you an expert on Linux, but it will definitely equip you with the knowledge base needed to become a pro in the Linux operating system.

Resources

How Linux Works 2nd Edition What Every Superuser Should Know by Brian Ward

https://askubuntu.com/questions/591787/how-can-display-a-message-on-terminal-when-open-it

https://bash.cyberciti.biz/guide/Quoting

https://blog.learningtree.com/how-to-practice-linux-skills-for-free/

https://likegeeks.com/bash-scripting-step-step-part2/#Nested-Loops

https://linuxacademy.com/blog/linux/conditions-in-bash-scripting-if-statements/

https://medium.com/quick-code/top-tutorials-to-learn-shell-scripting-on-linux-platform-c250f375e0e5

https://opensource.com/business/16/6/managing-passwords-security-linux

https://www.binarytides.com/linux-command-check-memory-usage/

https://www.computerhope.com/jargon/i/init.htm

https://www.cyberciti.biz/faq/bash-while-loop/

https://www.dedoimedo.com/computers/grub.html#mozTocId616834

https://www.digitalocean.com/community/tutorials/basic-linux-navigation-and-file-management

https://www.geeksforgeeks.org/basic-shell-commands-in-linux/

https://www.geeksforgeeks.org/break-command-in-linux-with-examples/

https://www.guru99.com/hacking-linux-systems.html

https://www.howtogeek.com/119340/htg-explains-what-runlevels-are-on-linux-and-how-to-use-them/

https://www.javatpoint.com/linux-error-redirection

https://www.javatpoint.com/linux-init

https://www.learnshell.org/en/Shell_Functions

https://www.linux.com/what-is-linux/

https://www.linuxtechi.com/10-tips-dmesg-command-linux-geeks/

https://www.techopedia.com/definition/3324/boot-loader

https://www.tecmint.com/how-to-hack-your-own-linux-system/

https://www.tecmint.com/understand-linux-shell-and-basic-shell-scripting-language-tips/

https://www.thegeekstuff.com/2011/02/linux-boot-process/

Linux Command Line and Shell Scripting Bible by Richard Blum

THE LINUX COMMAND LINE by William E . Shotts , J r .